MINERAL

LAND

RIGHTS

**THE ESSENTIAL GUIDE FOR LANDOWNERS
AND THE OIL AND GAS INDUSTRY**

LEVONNE LOUIE

MINERAL LAND RIGHTS

WHAT YOU NEED TO KNOW

Citrine PRESS

Copyright © 2014 by Levonne Louie

12 13 14 15 16   5 4 3 2 1

All rights reserved. No part of this book may be reproduced, stored in a retrieval system, or transmitted, in any form or by any means, without the prior written consent of the publisher or a licence from The Canadian Copyright Licensing Agency (Access Copyright). For a copyright licence, visit www.accesscopyright.ca or call toll free to 1-800-893-5777.

Citrine Press
Suite 2202, 1078 6th Avenue SW
Calgary AB
Canada T2P 5N6

Cataloguing data available from Library and Archives Canada
ISBN 978-0-9938037-0-3 (paperback)
ISBN 978-0-9938037-1-0 (ebook)

Publishing consulting by Jesse Finkelstein, Page Two Strategies
Editing by Lana Okerlund
Cover and text design by Peter Cocking
Printed and bound in Canada by Marquis

THIS BOOK IS not intended to provide legal advice, as I am not a lawyer. However, I have over thirty-five years of experience in the oil and gas industry that I would like to share. The information in this book will, I hope, provide a basic understanding of what mineral rights are and allow landowners and others interested in this industry to have an informed discussion about mineral rights.

Contents

Acknowledgements *1*

Introduction *3*

1 **Basic Information about the Oil and Gas Industry** *11*
2 **Basic Land Information** *21*
3 **Mineral Land Ownership** *33*
4 **Surface Land Ownership** *49*
5 **What You Can Do If You Hold Land Rights** *57*
6 **Key Clauses to Consider When Leasing Your Land** *75*
7 **The Leasing Process for Lands Owned by the Government** *97*
8 **After Your Land Has Been Leased** *103*
9 **When Land Changes Hands** *123*
10 **Final Thoughts** *125*

Sources of Further Information *129*

Frequently Used Terms *133*

Acknowledgements

THE IDEA OF writing this book came to me a few years ago. It was one thing to write the book, but it was a totally different process to see the book through to its final, published form.

I would like to thank my literary agent, Jesse Finkelstein of Page Two Strategies, for your support, patience, wisdom, and guidance as you helped me through the process. With your Page Two partner, Trena White, you have helped to demystify the strange, new, evolving world of publishing for me. Your assistance with the myriad details that I didn't even know about has been invaluable. In addition, your introduction to freelancers in your network who are tops in their fields has added to the professionalism evident in this final product. The team you assembled to work on my book is outstanding. I would not have been able to do this without you, Jesse.

A big thank you goes to my designer, Peter Cocking, for your patience and the creativity you applied to this book as well as to my brand and website design. Even though I often asked to see alternative versions of the designs you proposed, I inevitably returned to your original designs. Other members of my literary team that deserve a thank you are my editor, Lana Okerlund, and my proofreader, Jennifer Stewart. You've both helped to make the book better by adding your word skills to the project.

Thank you to David Younggren, Brian Skinner, Ross Harvey, Joan Dornian, and Judith Athaide for reading my book and agreeing to provide an endorsement. I greatly value the opinions of each of you, and I am humbled by your comments. Thank you to Sean Fairhurst for reading my book and providing your wisdom and guidance.

I owe a great deal of thanks to all the veteran landmen I have crossed paths with over the years for what I have learned from you. Your willingness to share your wisdom truly says a lot about the profession.

Finally, thank you to my daughter, Megan Mah, for your love and support. You inspire me to be the best person I can be, and you encourage me to follow my dreams.

Introduction

Why Have I Written This Book?

THE PURPOSE OF this book is to provide an overview of one of the basic components of the oil and gas industry: mineral land. Like any industry or profession, the oil and gas industry has a lot of jargon, but I have tried to create a book that is free of jargon and easy for the average reader to understand, whether or not you are in the oil and gas industry.

My original goal was to explain mineral land rights so that landowners could better understand what they have and what they can do with their mineral rights. That is still a major goal, but as I was writing the book and interacting with people in the oil and gas industry on a daily basis, I realized there is also a need within the industry for clarification of some basic concepts regarding mineral land. With this knowledge, people working in the industry can better understand the issues that can arise with mineral land and how these issues impact their jobs every day.

I will only briefly discuss certain aspects of the surface of the land, as there are many resources available to the surface landowner. There is far less information about mineral landholdings, and that is the focus of this book. One reason there is so little information for the mineral landowner is that few people actually own mineral rights compared to the number of people who own surface rights. In Canada, most mineral rights are held by the government, which is also known as the Crown.

My hope, however, is that if people learn about how this initial, essential piece of the oil and gas industry works, they will better understand the industry. Without mineral land rights, companies are not able to drill and explore for oil and gas. While it is true that we need other professionals such as geologists, geophysicists, engineers, and field people to actually find and extract oil and gas, they cannot do their jobs unless their companies hold mineral land rights. This book will help people become better-informed investors, employees, Lessors, Lessees, and working interest partners.

I have written this book primarily for landowners (both mineral and surface), but other readers will find valuable information here as well, including people who work in the oil and gas industry but do not work in the land area, First Nations communities and their administrators, regulatory bodies, people who work with oil and gas companies in advisory roles such as auditors and lawyers, and people who are interested in entering the industry (whether young people at the high school, college, or university level or people looking to make a career change). Each of these groups may have heard about mineral rights or land rights issues and how they impact the area they live, work, or are interested in, but this book will provide further information from an operational perspective.

About Me

Even though I have lived in Calgary, Alberta (the energy capital of Canada), since I was a year old, I basically knew nothing about the oil and gas industry when I was growing up. Like many young people of Asian descent, I focused my studies at the University of Calgary on a profession: in my case, medicine. About three and a half years into a four-year Bachelor of Science program, I decided that was not where I wanted to be. I had interests in so many areas that I didn't want to focus on one. Thankfully, the medical school interviewers saw this too, and I did not attend medical school. After completing my Bachelor of Science, I spent the next two years getting a Bachelor of Commerce degree.

The summer between those two years was very important to my future career, as I was introduced to the oil and gas industry. I spent the first half of that summer working with the federally sponsored Hire-a-Student program in Calgary, and I was fortunate to land a job for the last half of the summer with a major oil and gas firm in Calgary that was looking for a "mathematician." The job actually involved inputting data into a hand-held programmable calculator to arrive at numbers that were then input into a computer in order to do "static corrections on seismic data."

If that sounds foreign to you, that's exactly how it sounded to me at the time. However, I learned a lot that summer about geophysics and its application to finding oil and gas. When the summer was over, I continued working at the company thirty-five hours per week while completing my Bachelor of Commerce. During that time, I learned more about the oil and gas industry in general as well as the different areas in which a person could work. In the last semester of my degree program, I was fortunate to receive two job offers: a Junior Geophysicist position with the firm I was working for and a Junior Landman position with a major integrated oil and gas firm. It's always good to have choices.

I had only a general idea of what a landman did as a result of meeting some landmen at the company I worked for, whereas I was more familiar with the geophysicist position. My company was willing to train me in this area due to the fact that I had a Bachelor of Science. However, I chose to take the Junior Landman position, as I felt it would be a good opportunity to combine my technical skills and interests with my people skills and interests. This has proven to be true in my career and I have never regretted my decision.

I have spent over thirty-five years as a landman in one of the most exciting industries you can imagine. There are constant changes in the industry: whether they are advances in technology, the types of resources we pursue, how we extract the resources, or the people and their roles in the industry. I have worked for major integrated oil and gas companies (which not only explore for resources but refine them and sell them to the end user), for intermediate Explorers and Producers, for start-up junior companies, and in my own consulting company.

I have been fortunate to have had the opportunity to work in all areas of land: surface, administration, contracts, and negotiations. I have also worked in other areas of the oil and gas industry, such as natural gas marketing, hard rock minerals, corporate administration, and investor relations. I have worked closely with other landmen (mineral, surface, and brokers), geologists, geophysicists, engineers (drilling, completion, production, and reservoir), government regulators, gas marketers, accountants (production, joint interest, and controllers), bankers, community and stakeholder relations people, business developers, and a multitude of lawyers (oil and gas, corporate, securities, regulatory, real estate, and litigators, to name a few). Land is one of the few disciplines that allow an individual to interact with and learn from multiple areas within the energy industry, and I've taken advantage of that to learn from everyone I've interacted with.

Do You Know What I Know?

During my thirty-five-plus-year career, I have learned a number of things about the oil and gas industry in general and about land rights specifically.

As a landowner:

- Do you know exactly what you own? If not, do you know how to find out?

- If an oil and gas company approaches you to take a lease out on your land, are you prepared and do you know what questions you should ask?

- If you have a lease on your land, do you know what your rights and obligations are with respect to that lease?

- If you have a lease on your land but no well, do you know what the company may do to try to drill a well on your lease?

If you work in the oil and gas industry or are in an advisory role to the industry:

- Do you know the difference between mineral and surface rights and do you understand why you need both to drill a well? Do you know who gets a rental and who gets a royalty?

- Do you know why it takes so long to assemble mineral land for drilling?

- Do you know why your company has different working interests for different wells and how they came about?

- Do you know why your company has different partners for some of your wells?

These are just some of the questions this book will help readers answer.

Introduction 9

Geography: Where Do the Principles Covered in This Book Apply?

Most of the information I share in this book is based on my experiences in the Canadian oil and gas industry in western Canada. While I have worked with lands in other places in Canada and the United States, I have spent most of my career in the sandbox known as the Western Canadian Sedimentary Basin.

Many of the basic principles discussed in this book can be applied to the rest of Canada, to the United States, and potentially internationally and still make sense. Registry systems for land are often different in different places, but the basic concepts of land ownership are generally similar.

The information on the basic types of negotiations and deals between companies in the oil and gas industry also applies to many jurisdictions, although the scale of the deal might be different. For example, international deals are likely to be much larger than a deal in western Canada in terms of dollars committed, activity conducted, and the land base involved, but basic principles would still apply.

Final Introductory Thoughts

With better understanding of mineral land rights, perhaps there can be more cooperation among people who have an interest in the energy industry—both internal and external. People who work within an oil and gas company will gain knowledge that will help them understand the work that landmen do and how it impacts their area, which should help them do their own jobs better and improve their relationships and interactions within the industry, as they will have a better understanding of the exploration process. The landowner who owns mineral land rights or has received a mineral title from their grandparent or parent will have a better understanding of what they own and what they can do with it. My dream is that this short, informative book will be passed from generation to generation along with the title to the land.

1

Basic Information about the Oil and Gas Industry

How Does the Search for Oil and Gas Begin?

As with many things, the search for oil and gas often starts in the minds of people. Most often, these are people who have studied the solid and liquid parts of the earth, the history of the earth, and how the different processes that formed the earth may have led to an environment that allowed for the creation of various minerals and hydrocarbons on our planet. While many people who study the earth are known as earth scientists, the ones most often involved in searching for minerals or oil and gas are usually known as geologists.

Besides knowing about different types of rocks, geologists also need to understand what the environment looked like in past climates to create the rocks we see today. An important part of this is trying to determine what plant and animal life (including micro-organisms) might have existed in these past climates. This is important because, as the climate changed, certain organisms died and led to the formation of oil and gas. By knowing where these creatures may have existed, what was surrounding them in their environment, and what may have happened to the area over time, geologists try to predict where we might find oil and gas.

At the risk of offending my geologist colleagues, even if you have the best geologic model to predict where you will find oil and gas, you will not definitively know if you have oil and gas until you drill for it. Even then, there is no guarantee you can make money from the oil and gas you found by producing it. There are many stories in the oil and gas industry in which a well is a technical success from the geologist's point of view because oil and gas was discovered. However, due to many factors, the well may not be a commercial success. Such factors include low production rates, high costs to get the product to the surface, low prices received for the product, or the lack of a market. Any one or a combination of these and other factors could lead to a commercially unsuccessful well. We sometimes refer to these wells as technical successes but uneconomic.

However, I am getting ahead of myself. Once a geologist identifies an area that might have oil or gas, they need to acquire rights to the land in order to drill the prospect to see if oil or gas is actually present. If they don't have the land, it doesn't matter how good their idea is; they will not be able to drill to prove that their concept is correct.

Some companies choose to acquire land on speculation without any input from a geologist, but I much prefer acquiring land in an area where a geologist at least has an idea they wish to pursue. Having a geologist's input provides focus to the project. Otherwise, I could acquire a lot of land very cheaply, but if there is no possibility of oil and gas under the land, I may hold a lot of the proverbial "moose pasture."

Types of Companies in the Oil and Gas Industry

The companies involved in the oil and gas industry fall into two basic categories. There are companies that actually explore for and produce the oil and gas we use. I'll refer to these companies as Explorers and Producers. Just as important are the companies that support the exploration work by providing many of the services that Explorers and Producers need. I'll refer to this second group as Service Companies.

EXPLORERS AND PRODUCERS

There are many ways to consider the large number of companies within the Explorers and Producers group. We can look at the geographies in which they are exploring and operating. We can compare them in terms of their activities and how many activities in the oil and gas supply chain they are involved in—this is referred to as the degree of "integration." We can look to see if a company focuses on a particular type of product—oil or natural gas—or on a particular type of prospect. We can also study them in terms of the number of people they employ and the types of jobs that are done within the company. The goals set by the company often determine what the company ultimately looks like.

Geography

A multinational company operates in many countries. In the past, multinationals were typically very large companies with relatively large offices in each of the countries in which they operated. Today, this category includes smaller companies that have chosen to work internationally for various reasons. For example, a company may feel it can access more land for a better price or bring technology to develop resources cost-effectively in another country, or perhaps the company geologist has prior experience working in a particular country. Whatever the reason, a multinational company believes it can add more value for its shareholders by operating internationally.

There are also companies that operate in only one or two countries (for example, Canada and the United States, or Canada only). Often these are intermediate-sized companies that want to focus their resources, both money and people, on a select number of prospects in a limited number of jurisdictions.

Finally, a number of companies operate only in one particular area of a province or state. These companies typically are very small and have only a handful of employees. Some exploration companies consist of only one or two individuals—usually a geologist and possibly an engineer—who have spent the majority of their careers focused on a particular type of rock, sand, or geographical area and are experts on that particular "play." Since they have done very well in their careers exploring on that play, they stick to playing in their favourite sandbox.

Integration

Some companies focus on the exploration and production phase. In other words, they decide where they would like to drill, acquire the land, drill the well, apply the necessary processes to the well so the oil or gas can be brought to the surface (this is known as "completing" the well), produce the product, gather it, and then take it to a sales point where they can sell it to someone. This is known as the upstream part of the oil and gas business.

Other companies may take the oil and gas that has been produced from wells, move it from a sales point to a refinery or other type of facility, refine or separate it into products that can be used by you or me (such as gasoline, diesel, propane, ethane, or methane), transport the refined products to the end user market, and sell it to a distribution company for sale to the end user. This is known as the downstream part of the oil and gas business.

Most companies focus on either the upstream or downstream side. Large multinational companies active in both the upstream and downstream parts of the business are sometimes referred to as integrated companies. By necessity, integrated companies usually have many divisions involved in the process, from the identification of an exploration play all the way through to the sale of gasoline to you or me at the local gas station.

Type of Product

Some companies choose to focus on either natural gas or oil. They may even limit their focus to a depth—such as being a shallow gas producer—or a certain type of rock. Reasons for doing this will vary, but sometimes the company believes they have a specific expertise that will allow them to produce a particular product more effectively and efficiently than their competitors. While this might seem risky because it seems the company is putting all their eggs in one basket, a company choosing this strategy could diversify by choosing "baskets" in many different geographic areas.

Number of Employees and Types of Jobs within a Company

Companies such as the large integrated multinationals will often have thousands of employees performing many of the necessary functions in-house. These companies will often have their own geologists and geophysicists, surface and mineral landmen, construction departments, drilling and completion engineers, field operators, marketing departments, full accounting and audit personnel, health and safety personnel, and information technology and legal departments.

Intermediate and small companies often do not have the resources to fully staff all of these functions. Depending on how much capital they have to spend, they also may not have the activity level to justify carrying the overhead of all these departments. As in many industries, a company needs to weigh the costs and benefits of doing the work in-house or outsourcing it to an external individual or company. This is where Service Companies can come in to fill various needs.

A company can also decide whether to be an Operator of its properties or a Non-operator; this has an impact on the number of people it needs to employ. An Operator typically has a large interest in a property and any wells on that property. It often has the largest percentage interest in the property—though that isn't always the case—and operates the property on behalf of any other parties that have a smaller interest. Operators often have a good reputation for keeping costs low while maximizing the production and revenue from the land for the benefit of all parties holding an interest. Many companies like to be Operators because they have a sense of control over the properties in their portfolio.

A Non-operator typically has a smaller interest than the Operator and depends on the latter to operate the property effectively to keep costs down while maximizing the production and revenue from the land. The Non-operator also expects the Operator to manage functions such as maintaining good relations with surface landowners and reporting production to the government on behalf of all parties holding an interest in the land. Although the Non-operator still needs enough staff to monitor the activities of the Operator and to question those activities when appropriate, the Non-operator usually needs fewer employees than an Operator.

As you can see, Explorers and Producers can be grouped into a number of different categories and be described in many different ways.

SERVICE COMPANIES

Service Companies can be grouped in a similar way as Explorers and Producers. However, another way to view Service Companies is by the product or service they provide.

A company can provide multiple products or services to an Explorer and Producer or it can focus on just one. Some of the basic products that Service Companies provide are pipe for drilling or pipelining work, sand, water, and other fluids or gases for drilling or completion activities. Some of the basic services include surveying, drilling, completion, providing camps for remote locations, health and safety testing, training or monitoring, communications, public relations, investor relations, stakeholder relations, land brokerage, environmental services, audit services, and legal services.

The list of products and services is long because if someone can identify a need that is not being met by Explorers and Producers, whether they are large, intermediate, or small, that is a business opportunity. If a product or service is already being provided but someone has found a cheaper way to provide it, that is also an opportunity.

The list of Service Companies and the products and services they provide are evolving as the oil and gas industry evolves to meet the challenges it faces. As an example of a recent evolution, as new techniques were developed to release oil and gas from previously untapped, difficult-to-produce reservoirs, Service Companies were formed or expanded to provide the products necessary to unlock these rocks so the oil and gas can be released. With new technology, there is also a greater need to engage with stakeholders to explain the process and to address any concerns. As the Canadian oil and gas industry increases its presence on the global energy stage, many more opportunities will arise to fill new challenges, and I am sure we haven't even identified some of them yet.

Key Points in This Chapter

- Geologists study the rocks in the earth to try to predict where there might be oil and gas.

- Land must be secured in order to drill for oil and gas.

- Sometimes oil and gas is found but the costs to produce it exceed the revenue that can be earned from its sale.

- Explorers and Producers in the oil and gas industry come in many shapes and sizes. Some focus on the upstream side of the oil and gas business, some focus on the downstream side, and some do both.

- Service Companies provide many products and services to support the activities of Explorers and Producers.

- The energy industry is constantly evolving, and this will create many opportunities for those who are interested in this sector.

2

Basic Land Information

THERE IS A difference between surface land rights and mineral land rights. In order to drill a well to determine whether there is oil and/or gas in an area, a company has to have access to both types of rights.

A Short History of Freehold Lands

To understand the current mineral land situation, it is helpful to understand how mineral land ownership evolved in western Canada.

HUDSON'S BAY COMPANY

In 1670, King Charles II of England granted a charter to his cousin Prince Rupert and the latter's associates that resulted in the creation of the Governor and Company of

Adventurers of England Trading into Hudson's Bay—commonly known as the Hudson's Bay Company. Part of the grant gave the Hudson's Bay Company control of the lands that drained into Hudson's Bay, and these were known as Rupert's Land. This is important to the land discussion, because this amounted to almost 4 million square kilometres (1.5 million square miles) of western and northern Canada, which was more than 40 percent of the new nation. King Charles II believed this land was his to give because no other Christian monarch had claimed it. As a result of this initial grant by the King of England, lands owned by the government in Canada are often referred to as "Crown lands."

Through a Deed of Surrender dated November 19, 1869, the Hudson's Bay Company agreed to surrender Rupert's Land back to the Crown in exchange for a large sum of money and substantial landholdings. Rupert's Land was transferred back to the Crown and incorporated into the Dominion of Canada on July 15, 1870. In the provinces of Alberta and Saskatchewan, this gave the Hudson's Bay Company control of Section 8 and three-quarters of Section 26 in the majority of the Townships draining into Hudson's Bay.

Other than Rupert's Land, all land—both mineral and surface—was originally held by the government when Canada was a young nation. As exploration and settlement of this new land occurred, various rights were given to the railway companies as an incentive to build a cross-country rail line. Settlers who came west with the railway and homesteaded were granted mineral and surface rights by either the railway or the Crown. These lands, along with the lands granted to the Hudson's Bay Company out of the lands formerly known as Rupert's Land, are commonly known as freehold or fee simple lands.

In Canada, the Crown owns a high percentage of mineral rights, particularly in western Canada. Fee simple lands in the west and some other parts of the country typically followed the path of the railway.

Systems of Land Description

I'll briefly describe the different systems of land description so that the reader can understand the meaning of the information that appears on a land title. By knowing the basics of how land is described, you can approximate where a piece of land lies.

Different regions may have different ways of describing the land geographically. In Alberta, Saskatchewan, and parts of Manitoba and British Columbia, a grid system known as the Dominion Land Survey System (DLSS) is used. Key components of this system are Meridians, Ranges, Townships, and Sections. For example, the Fourth Meridian is located on the boundary between Alberta and Saskatchewan. Ranges are referred to as being West of the Fourth Meridian until the Fifth Meridian is reached. The Fifth Meridian roughly runs north-south through the city of Calgary and continues to run north-south approximately twenty kilometres (twelve miles) west of the western boundary of the city of Edmonton.

Townships run from Township 1 at the border between Canada and the United States up to Township 126 at the border between the provinces and the Northwest Territories (the sixtieth parallel). Each Township consists of thirty-six Sections that each measure 1.6 kilometres wide by 1.6 kilometres long (1 by 1 mile). So each Township is 9.6 by 9.6 kilometres (6 by 6 miles) in size. Each of the square Sections can be further divided into quarter Sections or legal subdivisions. Figure 1 illustrates how the DLSS has mapped out Alberta.

A small part of British Columbia around Fort St. John uses the DLSS and is known as the Peace River Block. The remainder of British Columbia uses the National Topographic System grid, and the Northwest Territories uses the Federal Permit System grid. Not much will be said about these survey systems in this book because the majority of the lands that individual landowners are concerned with are surveyed under the DLSS described above.

That said, a lot of recent activity in British Columbia is focused on the northeastern part of the province, so readers interested in knowing more about the National Topographic System can see how this system is applied in British Columbia by looking at Schedule 3 in the Petroleum and Natural Gas Grid Regulation (BC Reg. 536/2004), which can be found on the Province of British Columbia website (www.bclaws.ca; search by the regulation number noted above). The regulation also describes where the Peace River Block is located in the province.

If lands were surveyed as part of a town established by early settlers, sometimes known as homesteaders, there

Figure 1: Dominion land survey of Alberta

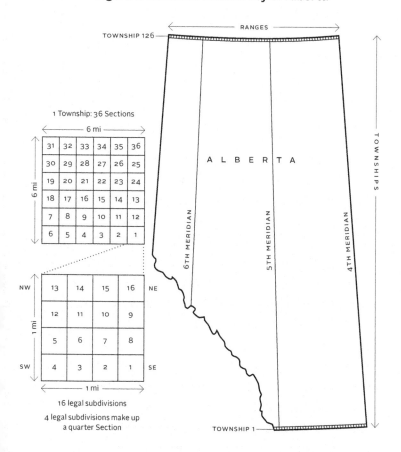

would be reference on the land title to a specific survey Plan with a registration number. The Plan would show certain Lot numbers, and these Lots were often established on either side of a river. Since there was no Global Positioning System in the early days, the survey would often contain language that described the physical surroundings. For example, the land description of a Lot might refer to the north boundary of a river. The St. Albert area of Alberta is one example where you can find this type of land description.

Land Titles and Rights

As a landowner, how do you confirm what you own? First, check the title to your land. A title contains key information such as the landowner's or landowners' name(s), the address for service, the number of hectares or acres contained in the title, and the land description, which includes the geographic location of the land using one of the survey systems described above. In cases where the land has been subdivided for development (common for surface rights but not as common for mineral rights), there will likely be a further description referencing a Plan number and Block and Lot numbers in the Plan.

If there is more than one landowner, the section that lists their names will also state what share each party owns and whether the landowners are joint tenants or tenants in common. Basically, with joint tenancy, if one of the parties dies, their share automatically goes to the other surviving parties. In a tenancy in common, each party holding an interest in the land can will their interest to someone else so that when they die, their interest goes to their beneficiaries or their estate. Joint tenancy is very common when a property is held by spouses. If one spouse dies before the other, the surviving spouse gets the property. Tenancy in common is more often seen when a property is held by siblings or unrelated parties. If one of the parties dies, their interest goes to whomever they've designated in their will.

A title also includes a description of the rights held within the area described geographically. Simplistically, if it says "all mines and minerals," the landowner on title owns mineral rights within the area described geographically. There could be some exclusions to the mines and minerals such as gold, silver, valuable stone, coal, petroleum, or any combination thereof. If there are exclusions on the title, another title or titles will cover those rights. If the title includes the words "excluding mines and minerals," the landowner on title owns the surface rights only. If there is no description of the rights held within the area described geographically, then the landowner owns both the surface rights and the mineral rights.

At the bottom of the title (or perhaps on the next page), there may be a list of caveats or other types of encumbrances that will affect the title. A caveat is simply a notice or warning to anyone reading the title that there may be some provisions or stipulations that affect the title. The caveator has some claimed interest in the land. Usually further digging is required to determine what the caveat actually relates to and how it impacts the title and any plans for the land. Common caveats on a title relating to surface rights are an agreement for sale, a mortgage, a Surface Lease, a utility right-of-way, or an Easement for a pipeline. Common caveats on a title relating to mineral rights are Petroleum and Natural Gas Leases or other agreements relating to the sharing of the proceeds from the mineral rights.

28 MINERAL LAND RIGHTS

Figure 2A: Example of a mineral title in Alberta

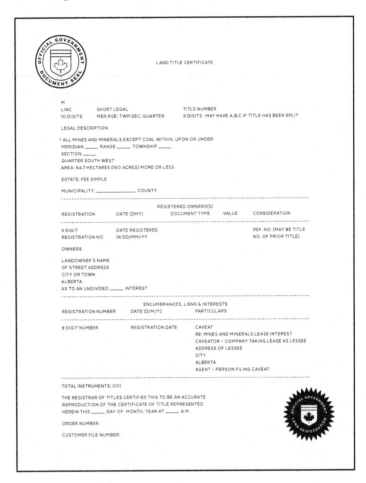

Figure 2 shows what a title in Alberta could look like and where specific information might be located. An example has been provided for both a surface title and a mineral title. Mineral land or mineral rights refers to the rights that are

Figure 2B: Example of a surface title in Alberta

below the surface of the land. These are sometimes referred to as mines and minerals on the land title, and they are the target of exploration, whether oil and gas exploration or mining exploration. If you compare land to a large layer cake,

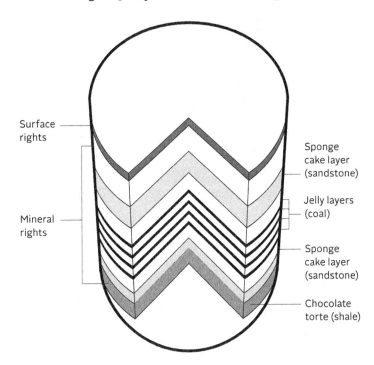

Figure 3: Layer cake view of land rights

Like a layer cake, mineral rights are composed of numerous layers. Each layer will have different characteristics depending on the type of material that makes up the layer.

---

the surface is the icing and the minerals are all those layers below the icing (see Figure 3). A large layer cake can have many different types of layers, such as sponge cake layers, ganache or torte layers, custard layers, and jelly layers. Similarly, there are different types of layers within the earth, such as sandstone layers, shale layers, and coal layers. Specific layers within the earth are sometimes referred to as formations or horizons.

Besides the difference in rights, there are two different types of land ownership. The government—whether of a municipality, province, state, or country—can own rights, either mineral or surface or both. In Canada, this is sometimes referred to as the Crown owning the lands or, simply, Crown lands. In Canada and in other jurisdictions, a government department usually has the responsibility of managing these lands on behalf of that government.

An individual, a group, or a company can also own land rights. This is sometimes referred to as fee simple or freehold land. The individual, group, or company is responsible for managing their land.

A given piece of land can have a combination of rights ownership, as shown in Figure 4.

Figure 4: Types of ownership

	SURFACE RIGHTS OWNER	MINERAL RIGHTS OWNER
Land 1	Government/Crown	Freehold/Fee Simple
Land 2	Government/Crown	Government/Crown
Land 3	Freehold/Fee Simple	Freehold/Fee Simple
Land 4	Freehold/Fee Simple	Government/Crown

As the matrix shows, there are many possible combinations of ownership and rights when one is talking about a piece of land.

Key Points in This Chapter

- There is a difference between surface rights and mineral rights.

- Certain lands in Canada were originally granted by King Charles II of England to a company that became the Hudson's Bay Company.

- The land originally owned by the Hudson's Bay Company was surrendered to the government of Canada in exchange for a large sum of money and selected lands. The land that the government purchased from the Hudson's Bay Company (other than the selected lands the company retained), together with other lands owned by the government, are known as Crown lands.

- Many individuals who own land rights today have them because their ancestors were homesteaders who came west with the railway. These lands, together with the lands retained by the Hudson's Bay Company, are known as freehold or fee simple lands.

- Land description systems vary from region to region. It is important to know what system is used in the area of interest.

- A land title contains key information about land ownership. Check your land title to see what you own.

- Land—whether owned by the government or by a freeholder, who could be an individual, a group, or a company—could include either surface rights, mineral rights, or both.

3

Mineral Land Ownership

IN ORDER TO drill for oil and/or gas, a company has to make sure it has leased or controls both mineral and surface rights.

It is very common in western Canada for the Crown to own both types of rights, particularly in more remote areas that are not heavily settled. This is one of the simplest combinations for companies to deal with. Even though different departments of the government might be involved, there are set parameters, guidelines, and regulations in place to deal with Crown lands.

It is more complicated for a company when an individual company or person owns the rights. Sometimes the same freehold owner controls both surface and mineral rights, but this is very unusual in western Canada due to the history of freehold lands. A more common, and potentially more complicated, scenario is where one individual owns the surface

Figure 5: Example showing mineral landowners holding 100 percent in a portion of a Section of land

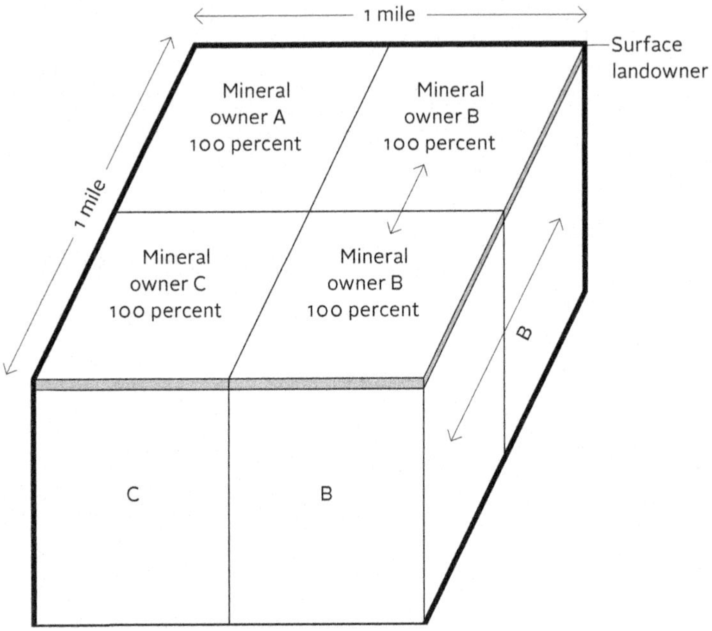

This example shows three landowners each holding a 100 percent interest in a portion of a Section (1 square mile).

---

rights and a different individual owns the mineral rights. This scenario becomes even more complicated when many individuals are involved in the surface rights and/or the mineral rights. Each individual owner has title to their land and has the freedom to decide what, if anything, they wish to do with it.

Examples of some of the complexities that occur with freehold lands are as follows:

Figure 6: Example showing a body of water on a Section of land (diagram shows mineral owners only)

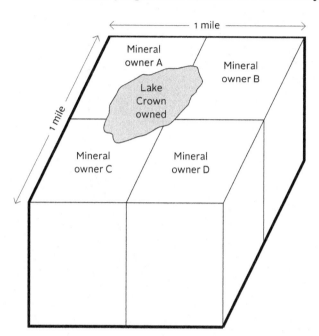

Each of mineral owners A, B, C, and D holds a portion of the quarter Section, and their titles will show the details of what they hold.

- A landowner owns 100 percent of a portion of a Section of land (a Section is generally 256 hectares/640 acres or 2.5 square kilometres/1 square mile in size in Alberta). This landowner may have only an interest in a quarter Section, a half Section, or a Lot in a subdivision Plan. See Figure 5.

- Bodies of water within a Section may have different ownership than the rest of the Section. For example, the Crown

36 MINERAL LAND RIGHTS

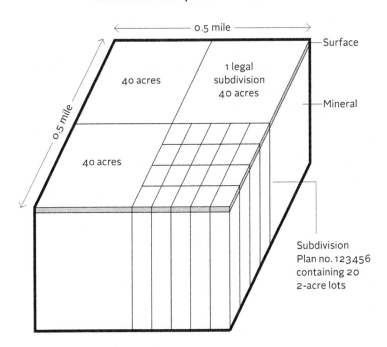

Figure 7: Example showing a subdivision in a quarter Section of land

Most often subdivision Plans involve surface rights only, but there are Plans that include surface rights and mineral rights.

may own a lake within a Section while the rest of the Section is held by individual owners. See Figure 6.

- Land has been subdivided for potential future development, and Plan numbers, Blocks, and Lots have become part of the land description. This is most commonly seen in surface rights titles, but I have seen a couple of instances where a subdivision Plan was applied to mineral rights titles. It is

Figure 8: Example showing multiple owners—six owners in the SW quarter Section (diagram shows mineral owners only)

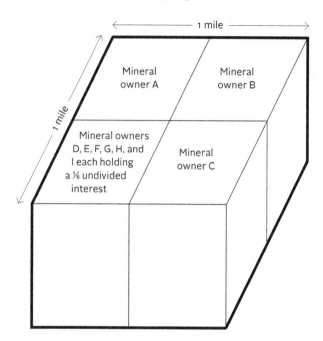

The six owners in the SW quarter each hold a ⅙ undivided interest and this will be shown on the titles.

---

hard to understand why someone would intentionally subdivide mineral rights, so perhaps these were an oversight when the subdivision was created. See Figure 7.

- A landowner owns an undivided interest in part of the land. For example, six individuals might each own a ⅙ undivided interest in the southwest quarter of a Section. See Figure 8.

Figure 9: Example showing split titles

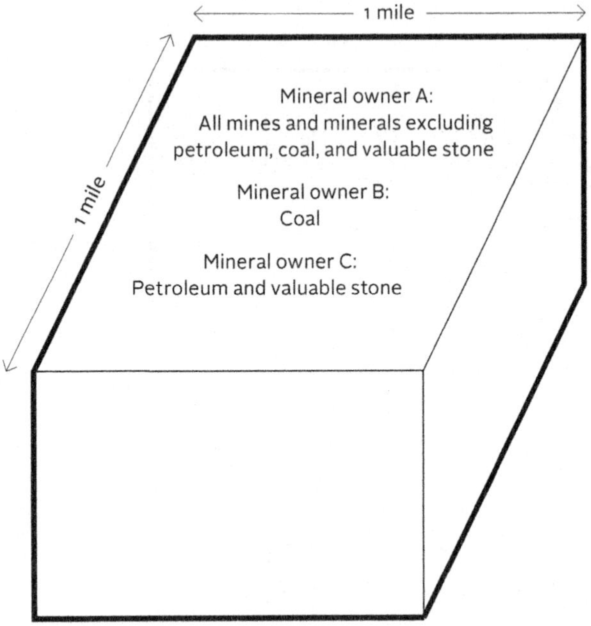

[Diagram of a rectangular section of land, 1 mile × 1 mile, labeled:]

Mineral owner A:
All mines and minerals excluding petroleum, coal, and valuable stone

Mineral owner B:
Coal

Mineral owner C:
Petroleum and valuable stone

Three owners hold different rights in a Section of land. The specific rights will be described on each of their titles.

- A landowner owns 100 percent of a Section of mineral rights that include all mines and minerals excluding petroleum, coal, and all valuable stone. Other parties own the title to the petroleum, coal, and valuable stone. See Figure 9.

How Did This Get to Be So Complex?

Let's look at a fictional individual, L, who owns a $1/16$ undivided interest in all mines and minerals excluding petroleum and coal in a quarter Section of land. Another party owns the title to the petroleum and coal. Here are some of the circumstances that could have created this ownership scenario:

- L's great-grandfather came out west when the railway was built. He was enticed to leave his home in eastern Canada as the railway was offering free land to anyone prepared to work the land and settle in the west. He received a quarter Section of land (64 hectares/160 acres) and his title showed he had all mines and minerals excluding petroleum and coal. The railway company kept title to these resources as they needed them to fuel their locomotives.

- L's great-grandfather worked the land hard, married, and had a large family. That generation often had large families so that there were more hands to work the farm. When L's great-grandfather died, he left the land to his oldest son, L's grandfather. So far, this seems simple.

- L's grandfather also worked hard, married, and had a large family. When L's grandfather died, he left the farm (i.e., the surface rights) to his oldest son (L's uncle) and the mineral rights to his remaining eight children (including L's father). So L's uncle had the family farm and L's dad and his other seven siblings each held a $1/8$ undivided interest in the mineral rights.

Figure 10: Example of how it can get so complicated

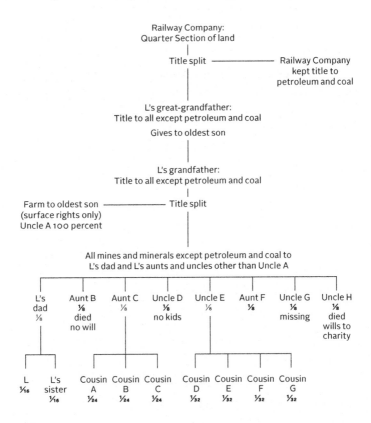

How L got a 1/16 interest in a quarter Section of mineral rights. Interests that are in bold type show the current mineral interests in the quarter Section.

- When L's dad died, he passed on his mineral rights to each of his two kids. Now L and his sister each have a 1/16 undivided interest in all mines and minerals excluding petroleum and coal in this quarter Section of land.

- The other ⅞ interest in the mineral rights can also have a very complicated chain of title. One of L's aunts decided to leave her share to her three children. Each of these children now holds a 1/24 undivided interest in the mineral rights. One of L's uncles decided to leave his share to his four children, who now each hold a 1/32 undivided interest in the mineral rights. Another of L's uncles decided to seek his fortune elsewhere and no one in the family has heard from him for years. Another of L's aunts died with no family and no will. See Figure 10.

As you can see, the freehold title situation can get very complicated very quickly. If all parties are known to each other and trust each other, they could appoint a party to represent their interest. If some of the parties could get together to appoint someone to represent their group, this makes it easier for a company to negotiate with the group and increases the likelihood that a company will make the effort to get leases from all parties so the land can be explored. The company needs to weigh the costs of getting leases from all parties against what it hopes to find and the expected gain from selling the product, assuming it is successful.

In cases where parties are missing (such as Uncle G in the example above), companies will sometimes hire private investigators to try to locate them. If the company has reached an agreement with the rest of the parties and the missing party still has not been located, the company can apply to the regulator to formally pool the lands to complete the drilling spacing unit, which will allow it to apply for a well licence. (There is more discussion later in this book about why all parties need to be contacted.)

If a Pooling Order is granted, the Public Trustee looks after the interests of the missing party on their behalf. The Public Trustee sets up an account for the missing party, and the company pays any proceeds owing to that party to the "Public Trustee in trust for the name of the missing party." If the party shows up at some point in the future and finds out that they own a portion of land and that there has been activity on it, they can contact the office of the Public Trustee to see what is being held for them.

I have actually been involved in a situation in which I had to hire a private investigator to try to locate an individual. The individual's name was on a very old title from the 1940s, and the address given for them on the title no longer existed. We had secured leases from the rest of the parties holding an interest in the land and were just missing this one individual. None of the others holding an interest in the land knew the individual, and we suspected that he may have been a distant relative from a long-forgotten branch of the family. The private investigator's report showed the individual had moved from one province to another in Canada and then to the United States. The investigator was able to track him through two states before, as they say, the trail went cold. Since we were unable to find the individual, we applied to the provincial regulator for a Pooling Order so we could apply for a well licence to drill on the lands. In support of the Pooling Order, we had to show all our efforts to locate the individual, including a copy of the private investigator's report. A Pooling Order was granted and an account was set up with the Public Trustee in the event that this individual or his heirs surfaced in the future.

Title Searches: How to Find Out Who Owns What

To determine who owns what, a party has to search all the titles on the lands of interest. We are fortunate in Alberta to have a central registry system known as the Land Titles Office. It is based on a principle known as the Torrens title system, and through legislation (the Alberta Land Titles Act), the definitive title is what is shown in the registry.

Searching a title used to be a relatively simple process when it was centralized by the provincial government. You would simply pay a visit or send a form to the North (located in Edmonton) or South (located in Calgary) Land Titles Office, depending on the location of the lands you were interested in. If you needed help, there were often people called document examiners in the office who could help ensure that you requested the right information. In the same general offices you could request copies of survey plans of specific developments or subdivisions.

As part of my training as a Junior Landman, I spent six months working in Edmonton for the Surface Land Department of a major multinational, integrated Explorer and Producer. As the rookie in the office, one of my jobs was to submit and pick up all of our land title searches. I remember going into the North Land Titles Office located a couple of blocks north of our Jasper Avenue office. It was housed in a very old, likely historic, building that was cavernous inside and had amazing architecture. I had to find out where to submit our search requests and then find our mailbox (we had our own since we were such a frequent client) to pick up the search results. Since we were quite busy, I needed to visit the office once and sometimes twice a day. The advancement of computers and the ability of companies to request searches online make the daily walk to the Land Titles Office unnecessary and obsolete. Sometimes I think that's a pity, as those daily walks allowed me to get out of the office and into the summer sun for a while!

The government privatized this service a number of years ago. Now an individual needs to go into a registry office and, for a fee, request a search of the title (mineral, surface, or both) on a piece of land. Companies can establish an account with a registry office and request their searches online. These privately owned registry offices are listed in the phone book or online and are widely distributed through Alberta. Titles can be accessed at these registry offices no matter what part of the province the lands of interest are located in.

In other jurisdictions both in Canada and the United States, records are often kept in the local courthouses or county seats. Finding out who definitively owns a particular tract of land will involve going back through the records in the local courthouses and looking at all the transfers that have occurred on that piece of land. This is sometimes referred to as a historical title opinion or historical title search. Only when the title chain is complete and all the right owners have been identified can a company start to make leasing approaches to those parties.

Why Do All the Parties Need to Be Involved Before a Company Can Drill a Well?

Many jurisdictions have established regulations that determine how much land a company has to have under its control before it can apply for a licence to drill a well. The required drilling spacing unit (DSU) is determined using geological and engineering principles to predict the optimal spacing to efficiently produce a formation so as to achieve the maximum production from a well. The objective of the DSU is to have the fewest wells on a Section to extract as much of the resource as possible out of that formation.

Certain formations may need more wells per Section, and sometimes these can be handled by special application to the regulator. Historically in Alberta and much of western Canada, the standard DSU for a vertical oil well was a quarter Section and for a vertical gas well was a full Section. This was the area that the regulator felt could be effectively captured by one well. These standard DSUs for oil and gas were put in place for what typically are known as conventional reservoirs, and they still apply when dealing with these types of formations. Unconventional reservoirs may require either more wells per Section or horizontal wells to effectively produce the resource. Regulators are adapting to address these more recent developments by allowing an increased number of wells in a DSU, thereby increasing the density of wells, as well as by using other methods for determining the appropriate DSU for a horizontal well. A discussion about conventional and unconventional reservoirs can be found in Chapter 6.

What this means is that companies are required to show or state that they have control of the DSU before they will be granted a licence to drill a well, and that they have common ownership before they can produce a well. In the case of a gas well, a company has to have control of the mineral rights for the entire Section of land. In the case of an oil well, a company has to show it has control of a quarter Section of land. Once the company has control of all mineral rights for a particular DSU, it effectively combines these rights so that the landowners share in the production from the DSU proportionate to their share of the land. A form of production-sharing agreement or Pooling Agreement may be required.

What is meant by proportionate share is best described using a simple example. There are two landowners, A and B. Landowner A holds a title for 16 hectares (40 acres) of mineral rights on a particular quarter Section of land. Landowner B holds a title for 48 hectares (120 acres) of mineral rights on the same quarter Section of land. Together these two titles make up the total quarter Section of land.

The DSU for an oil well is a quarter Section, and a company wishes to drill for oil on this quarter Section, 25 percent of which is held by A and 75 percent by B. The company gets a mineral lease from A and a separate mineral lease from B and drills a successful oil well. Landowner A will receive a royalty payment that is calculated by multiplying 25 percent of the production from the well by the royalty rate they negotiated with the company (less any negotiated deductions). Landowner B will receive a royalty payment that is calculated by multiplying 75 percent of the production from the well by the royalty rate they negotiated with the company (less any negotiated deductions). Note that the royalty rates for each lease are not necessarily the same; they depend upon what each of the landowners was able to negotiate with the company for their particular lease.

Sometimes a company is missing only a small portion of the land to complete a DSU. This may be because a party cannot be located or a party does not wish to lease or contribute the lands it has under its control. When this happens in Alberta, the company can apply to the regulator for a Pooling Order. As described earlier in this chapter, to apply for a Pooling Order, the company must provide details of all the efforts it has made to complete a DSU; this is not a frivolous process. Once a Pooling Order is granted, the company can then apply for its well licence, and the Pooling Order establishes a mechanism to pay the parties who either were missing (with payment made to the Public Trustee) or did not wish to contribute the land under their control.

Our fictional landowner, L, holds a $1/16$ interest in a quarter Section of mineral rights. A company wanting to drill a gas well on L's land needs to find and negotiate leases with the landowners of the remaining $15/16$ of that quarter Section as well as the three remaining quarter Sections to complete the DSU for drilling a gas well. In addition, the company has to negotiate a Surface Lease from the descendants of L's uncle in order to put in the wellsite and access road. The Surface Lease would be for only one to two hectares (two to five acres); the size depends on the type of equipment that will be on the site and the length of the access road, if any. Only when the company has mineral leases from all mineral owners and a Surface Lease from the surface owner is it in a position to apply for a well licence. It can be a time-consuming, labour-intensive exercise to identify and then secure a lease from all landowners.

Key Points in This Chapter

- Situations in which the Crown owns both mineral and surface rights are the easiest for oil and gas companies to deal with.

- Mineral and surface rights for freehold lands tend to be held by different owners, and can sometimes be very complex. Know what you own.

- In the provinces of western Canada, a company needs to show that it has control over a complete drilling spacing unit (DSU) before it can apply for a well licence.

- If a landowner cannot be located, despite the company's best efforts, the company can apply to the regulator for a Pooling Order.

- When a landowner receives a royalty on a lease they have negotiated, the royalty rate is paid on their proportionate share of production from the DSU. If the land amounts to 25 percent of the DSU, the royalty rate will be applied to 25 percent of the production from the DSU.

4

Surface Land Ownership

THIS CHAPTER PROVIDES a brief description of surface rights and how the oil and gas industry impacts surface landowners. This is a brief segment mainly because so much information is already available about surface rights, and I have listed a few key resources at the end of this book. One reason that so much industry material focuses on surface rights is because the surface is what the public sees in a field. More importantly, in western Canada, more people hold title to surface rights than to mineral rights. As oil and gas activity comes into an area, surface landowners tend to be most impacted by drilling, pipelining, and associated activities.

Because of the large amount of material on surface rights, the focus of this book is on mineral rights. However, the following is a brief summary of the process that happens with a surface landowner when a company decides to drill on his or her land.

Crown Surface Rights

The Crown can hold surface rights, and this is typically the case in areas where there was not a lot of settlement. For Crown surface rights, there is an established process whereby a company submits a survey plan showing its proposed activity and pays a set fee for the application. The Crown reviews the application, coordinates any necessary consultation, and, if the application is judged to be in the best interests of all parties involved, grants the application. When the surface landowner is the Crown, there is generally a set fee and then a rental based on the amount of land covered by the Surface Lease. Fees and rentals tend to be established by regulation so all parties have an idea of the costs involved.

Freehold Surface Rights

The process tends to become more complex when an individual owns the surface rights instead of the Crown. For a mineral rights holder to access the mineral rights, they need to access the surface rights. Often an access road and wellsite are required in addition to a right-of-way for a pipeline, particularly if the product is natural gas. If the product is oil, it can be stored in tanks on the Surface Lease until there is sufficient quantity to be trucked off the lease site at an economical price.

    The wellsite and access road are typically held in the form of a Surface Lease. A Right-of-Way Agreement or Easement is used for the pipeline. Leases vary in size, but companies will take a Surface Lease large enough so that their trucks and equipment do not encroach on unleased land. If companies are drilling for a formation that can be produced from a single well, it is not unusual to lease a 15-metre (50-foot) access road and a 100- by 100-metre (330- by 330-foot) wellsite. Once the well has been drilled, the company will often allow the landowner to farm over portions of the leased land. For example, a landowner may be able to farm right up to a small fenced area that contains the wellhead (a pipe sticking out of the ground with some valves on it).

A Surface Lease is also used for a facility such as a compressor station, where the gas from an area is gathered and compressed, which increases the pressure of the gas so it can enter a larger pipeline taking the gas to a sales point. Some gas is produced from wells at very low pressure. Unless it is given a boost by compression, it will not be able to enter the higher-pressure sales line.

If you are a surface landowner and you negotiate a Surface Lease, you will get a first-year consideration (sometimes referred to as a bonus) as well as an annual rental. Components making up the first-year consideration include land value, adverse effect, nuisance, inconvenience, noise, and loss of use. The annual rental components include adverse effect, nuisance, inconvenience, noise, and loss of use. These figures are all negotiated between you and the company.

There is also a provision for periodic review of the rental (sometimes legislated), and special conditions may be included with the Surface Lease. For example, one special condition may be that the company does not enter the land until the crops have come off. If there are special conditions, it is important they be written down so all parties share a clear understanding of them.

Once a well has been drilled and is capable of production, a pipeline is sometimes necessary, particularly for natural gas. An Easement or Right-of-Way Agreement gives the grantee the right to lay a pipe in a specified right-of-way. Sometimes permission is granted to lay more than one pipeline in the right-of-way, but this would need to be specified in the agreement. The company makes a one-time payment to the landowner for a Right-of-Way Agreement, the components of which are land value, adverse effect, nuisance, inconvenience, noise, loss of use, and impact on remaining lands. The company is also responsible for any damages that occur on land not included in the Surface Lease or the Right-of-Way Agreement. The logic for a one-time payment is that the landowner can work the land over the right-of-way after the pipe is in the ground. If the company needs to come back onto the right-of-way to do some work in the future, it may have to pay again, depending on what the document says.

Surface Leases and Right-of-Way Agreements evolve over time. As with any document you are asked to sign, it is important to understand the various components of the agreement. Both you and the company need to understand your rights and obligations under the documents being signed.

Sometimes a landowner agrees to have a well on their land and to where the well will be placed, but does not agree on the lease payment amount. In this case, a body in Alberta known as the Surface Rights Board can hold a compensation hearing to determine fair compensation for both parties. British Columbia and Saskatchewan have similar bodies to assist the parties.

If you are a surface landowner who does not have a well on your land, but you see a lot of wells around your area and wish to have one too, you can contact the company that is exploring around you to indicate your interest. The company name and phone number should be on the well signs for the other wells. Companies are always interested in knowing where they have a willing surface landowner. Before you make the call, find out who you are dealing with and what their reputation is by researching them on the Internet or simply asking your neighbours.

However, just because you've offered your land as a possible drilling site does not mean that you will get a well on your land. There may be a reason you have not been approached. Perhaps the mineral rights title(s) underlying your land are complicated and the company has not been able to lease all the mineral rights. Until it has all the mineral rights leased or under control for the regulated DSU, the company is not able to proceed. Another factor is whether the reservoir it is exploring for is on your land. Geologically, the formation the company is interested in may not be present under your land. Another factor is the price the company can get for the oil or gas it finds. Given the current and projected prices, is it worth it for the company to drill for the product? These are just some of the things a company needs to consider before talking to a surface landowner.

As you learned in an earlier chapter, the surface landowner is often different than the person or company that owns the mineral rights. Sometimes these different landowners are related. I had the good fortune early in my career of receiving my surface land training from surface landmen who had twenty-five to thirty-five years of experience. The best advice these veteran landmen gave me was to never get between a surface landowner and a mineral landowner, especially if they were from the same family.

If you think about it, you will realize it is a no-win situation for the person in the middle. The surface landowner receives a bonus consideration and an annual rental for having a well on their land. Even though they are paid for it, they deal with any noise, dust, and other inconveniences of having that well. The mineral landowner, who may not even live in the area, receives a bonus consideration and a royalty for having a well on their land. If the company successfully drills and produces the well, the mineral landowner will receive monthly royalty cheques. Who would you rather be—the surface landowner or the mineral landowner? Perhaps you now understand why it is good advice to never get in the middle.

Surface rights issues can become complicated, and these complications are not within the scope of this book. The reader is invited to check out the resources at the back of the book for further information.

Key Points in This Chapter

- There are many resources available for the surface landowner and not many available for the mineral landowner.

- It is relatively easy to get a Surface Lease when the Crown holds the lands. Many of the fees and rentals are established and there is a process in place for the application.

- The terms of Surface Leases and Right-of-Way or Easement agreements with freehold landowners are all negotiated.

- In Alberta, if the surface landowner is okay with the idea of having a well on their land and with the location of the well, but is not happy with the compensation being offered, they can go to the Surface Rights Board for a compensation hearing.

- It is important for parties to keep the communication lines open when negotiating a lease and after the lease has been signed. This applies to many areas covered by this book.

5

What You Can Do If You Hold Land Rights

IT IS VERY important to determine if you hold title to land rights on the surface of the land, or the mines and minerals below the surface of the land, or both. Some of the things you can do with your land are the same no matter if you hold mineral or surface rights. For example, as a landowner of mineral rights or surface rights, you can usually do the following:

- Sell your land

- Explore and develop your land

- Lease your land to someone else to develop or work for you

- Do nothing now and, upon your death, pass the land through a will to your spouse, children, siblings, or others, unless you hold the land with someone as joint tenants. Your interest in the land can also be assigned to someone before your death.

Let's look at the first three of these scenarios in a little more detail.

Sell Your Land

No matter if you are a mineral landowner or a surface landowner, you can sell your land at any time, subject to any existing encumbrances on the title of your land. Encumbrances on a surface title might include a mortgage, an existing lease such as a Surface Lease or a grazing lease, a subdivision Plan, or an Easement or right-of-way covering power lines, pipelines, or roadways across your property. Valuation of a surface property will take into account the appraised market value, the use of the property, any improvements on the land, and whether it is developed, cultivated, or pasture. A certified appraiser would be the best person to estimate the value of your land if you want to sell it.

If you are a mineral landowner, you might have encumbrances on your title such as an existing Petroleum and Natural Gas Lease(s) or Gross Royalty Trust certificates. Valuation of the mineral land can be a little more difficult. The presence or lack of drilling activity around your land may have an impact on the value of your mineral rights. If there are numerous producing wells around your land, it could be worth more than if it were surrounded by abandoned wells. The land could also be worth less if parties believe that minerals have been drained from your Section by surrounding production. If the surrounding wells are producing oil or natural gas from unconventional reservoirs such as tight sands, coals, or shales, however, surrounding production will likely not have caused any drainage from your Section due to the characteristics of the rock the oil or natural gas is coming from.

To place a value on your land, you can hire a reservoir engineer or a reservoir engineering company. If there is production from your land, they will look at some or all of the following factors:

- How much has already been produced?
- Approximately how much is left to be produced from the producing horizons?
- How long will it take to produce the remaining product?
- Are there any other prospective horizons under your land? If so, what might they be expected to produce and over what period?
- What prices are expected to be received for the product?
- What royalty rate are you getting on the current production?
- What is all this worth in today's dollars?

If there is no current production on your land, they will then look at what may be under your land and apply some of the questions noted above.

As you can see, many factors go into calculating what your mineral rights may be worth.

If someone comes knocking who wants to buy your mineral rights, they might see something there that no one else sees. As we figure out more ways to use technology to produce oil and gas, lands that were formerly thought to be tapped out or drained may still produce from other formations.

If you want to sell your land and you have a potential buyer, remember there is no strict answer as to what the price should be. If you don't want to hire someone to give you a valuation and you do not know anyone in the industry who does this type of calculation on a regular basis, you might need to come up with a number yourself.

If the buyer and the seller are both happy with the agreed price, then that is the right price.

Be reasonable in your position; the company or individual offering to purchase your land is taking a gamble that there is something there. Remember that you are trading the future royalty payments you would receive if a company were to lease your land and successfully drill an economic well for the dollars you are receiving now.

It is extremely important that you read your title carefully to determine if there are any exclusions to your mineral rights. Common exclusions include gold, silver, and valuable stone. Occasionally, depending on how the lands became freehold mineral rights, petroleum and/or coal may be excluded. This is particularly true in the case where settlers got their interest from the railway. Petroleum and coal were often excluded from grants to settlers because the railway needed these commodities to run locomotives. If you decide to sell your land, make sure you know what you are selling.

Explore and Develop Your Land Yourself

Often, a surface landowner "develops" their land by farming it, whether they live on it or not. They could also lease it to someone else to farm or allow someone to put animals on the land to graze on it. If the land is close to an urban centre, development might mean subdividing the land into Lots and then selling individual Lots. The main point here is that the surface landowner can see what they have to work with and what they can develop.

As a mineral landowner, you may want to be involved in developing your mineral rights. Unless you have some technical knowledge or access to technical knowledge, this is often difficult to do for a variety of reasons, and even if you have or can find the knowledge and expertise, it can be an expensive venture.

First, if this is the only land that you have, you have to have a high tolerance for risk. There is no guarantee that there will be mines and minerals in your land. You have to determine where to drill on your land and acquire a Surface Lease for your wellsite (assuming you do not own the surface rights). The well has to be drilled without any problems into the right spot to find the right formation or reservoir.

Once the reservoir has been found and it appears to contain hydrocarbons (oil or gas), certain processes may need to be applied to the reservoir for the oil or gas to be produced (referred to as "completing" a well). Even if there are producing wells all around your property, certain processes may need to be applied to the rock on your land to increase the chances that you will get a similar type of well as the one across your fenceline.

Even if you do find oil and/or gas on your land, can it be brought to the surface and to the market economically? You first have to determine who you will sell your oil or gas to. With oil, once you have found a buyer, you can truck it to a site for processing. With gas, you will have to pipeline it into a gathering system to be taken to a gas plant for processing and/or compression. If your gas is at very low pressure, you may need to add compression to get it into the main line, and you may need to strip out water and any contaminants before it will be accepted. Once you have added up all the costs, are you going to make any money?

Second, if you are comfortable with the level of risk and have a lot of money to spend, you will need to deal with the regulations associated with drilling a well. First and foremost, you need to be able to show the regulator that you control the mineral rights under the DSU. As discussed earlier, in many jurisdictions in western Canada, a DSU is a full Section (256 hectares/640 acres) if you are planning to drill a gas well and a quarter Section (64 hectares/160 acres) if you are planning to drill an oil well.

If you do not have all the rights in the required DSU, you will need to contact the remaining landowners and either get leases from them (which would include negotiating the basic items of term, royalty, etc.) or negotiate a pooling arrangement with them that will allow you to have access to the full DSU. Even if the other landowners agree to pool their lands to complete the DSU, you will need to determine whether they wish to participate in the drilling of a well. The Pooling Agreement could stipulate how other parties will share in the cost of drilling a well and how they will split the proceeds.

Once the rights in the necessary DSU are acquired or leased, you have to negotiate surface access with the surface rights owner in order to drill the well. Numerous regulatory requirements also have to be satisfied to secure a well licence to drill. Most of these regulations are in place to ensure that a competent Operator drills the well in a safe manner. The regulator might also consider whether the Operator of the proposed well has the financial capability to conduct all necessary operations, including the costs of abandoning the well should it be unsuccessful in finding oil or gas.

Third, even if you have extremely deep pockets, you need to be comfortable with putting your money into this one opportunity to find commercial production on your mineral rights. This assumes you have only a limited amount of land. Companies can spread their risk by drilling several wells in several different areas and potentially on several different types of prospects (for example, drilling on a conventional gas play in one area and an unconventional oil play in another area). Successful wells in one area may partially offset poor drilling results in another. Certain sections of a prospect may have a higher chance of success than other sections within the same prospect.

If it is too complicated, costly, and/or risky for you to explore and develop your own land, what are you going to do? Find someone else, like an oil and gas company, to explore and develop the rights for you by granting them a freehold mineral lease.

Lease Your Land

As either a surface landowner or a mineral landowner, you can lease your land to someone else to develop. As a surface landowner, you can lease your land to someone else to graze their cattle or to farm. With respect to oil and gas operations, in most Canadian jurisdictions, a mineral owner who wishes to access mineral rights below the surface has to seek permission from the surface owner to cross the land and drill a well. Under English common law, a surface landowner cannot stop a mineral landowner from accessing their minerals. However, the surface landowner is entitled to fair compensation. In many jurisdictions, regulatory boards assist in arbitrating the compensation issue. If the parties cannot agree on the location of the wellbore, another regulatory body may become involved in a hearing. Surface rights were discussed in Chapter 4, and more information is available from the sources identified at the end of this book.

As a mineral landowner, you can lease your rights to a company to explore your land and potentially drill a well to find and produce petroleum substances. In exchange for granting the lease, you will receive an initial consideration based on how many acres are leased. Another key component of a mineral landowner's compensation is the royalty. The royalty represents the landowner's share of the minerals being produced.

If the company is successful and finds a productive well, you will receive value from your land. If the company does not have success and finds only a dry hole, your mineral rights will likely return to you. You may be able to lease them to another company going after a different formation or using different technology to explore the same formation.

In the past, Lessors (mineral landowners) would typically lease their land for a five-year term, a 12.5 percent royalty, and a per-acre bonus consideration that was the going rate in the area. As the industry has grown and more wells have been drilled, landowners have become better informed and are raising other factors in negotiations, such as what is happening on the other side of the fence and what companies are pursuing.

The next sections discuss how the leasing process works, what is involved, factors that a company might consider when pursuing a Petroleum and Natural Gas Lease, and factors that a landowner should consider when approached by a company to lease their mineral rights. Understanding the considerations on both sides should help the parties to reach an agreement that is of benefit to both. Although I provide some examples, you need to understand that these types of negotiations are generally confidential, and not every Petroleum and Natural Gas Lease will have the same terms. Like any negotiation, the interests of both parties need to be understood to arrive at a mutually satisfactory agreement.

TO WHOM DO YOU LEASE AND HOW DO YOU FIND THEM?

By granting a Petroleum and Natural Gas Lease to a company, your hope as a mineral landowner is that the company will explore on the land and, if it chooses, drill into the mineral rights to determine if there is oil and/or gas present at no cost or risk to you. If economically productive oil or gas is found, you will share in the resource by way of the royalty.

As a landowner, you want to lease to a company that has a high probability of exploring and drilling on the land during the term of the lease. Another important consideration is the reputation of the company you are considering. Here are some ideas to identify likely leasing candidates:

- Find out the names of companies currently developing mineral rights nearby. The well signs in the area will include company names and contact information.

- If you know someone who works in the industry, ask them to check who owns or controls the mineral rights on nearby land. While they may not be able to see who the mineral landowners are without searching the land titles, they can likely find out the names of companies that have taken leases from nearby landowners. They can also identify the licenced Operator of any nearby wells.

- Once you have identified who might be active in the area, check out their websites. If a number of companies are in the area, gather some information to decide which one you want to work with. Does each company have the financial capacity and technical personnel to drill the well and do all the things necessary to produce the well? What is the reputation of the company and its people? If you know any surface landowners in the area, ask them about their experiences with the different companies. They will often have opinions about who they like to deal with and who they would prefer not to deal with.

Companies will often use brokers to acquire leases on their behalf—both for surface leasing and mineral leasing.

Companies do this to remain anonymous and to maintain a competitive advantage. This most often occurs at Crown land sales. In dealing with individual landowners, companies often use a broker simply because it is not economic for them to hire a full-time employee to lease land for them, particularly if they are in areas where there is not a lot of freehold land. It is more cost-efficient to use a land brokerage firm that has many landmen on staff and charges out by the hour or project.

If you are approached by a broker, you can ask them who they are working for; however, they may or may not give you this information. If the land broker is unable to divulge who their client is, you can choose not to lease your land until that information is available. The result of this may be that your land is not one of the first pieces of land drilled, but if the company has success in the area, there is a good chance they will be back to talk to you.

Brokers also have a reputation to maintain in the industry and with landowners, so if you are comfortable leasing to the land brokerage company regardless of whether you know the name of the underlying Explorer and Producer, the lease can name you as the Lessor and the brokerage company as the Lessee. At some point in the future, the land brokerage company might assign the lease to the company actually doing the work.

Once you've identified one or more companies or land brokers active in the area and decided whom you might want to work with, contact them to let them know your land is available for lease. This may mean contacting the company directly or contacting the broker working for the company.

You may not get a response right away if there is not a lot of activity in the area. The companies you contact have to evaluate what might be contained in your rights. They also need to consider the amount of resource that might be there, how much it will cost to get it out, and what they could sell it for before they decide whether to lease your land. Sometimes they go through this exercise before they lease your land. Other times they may lease your land and go through the details of geology and economics afterward.

Whether you are trying to identify who might be interested in your land or you get an unexpected phone call about leasing it, you need to do your homework like you would in any other business deal. When signing a freehold mineral lease or Petroleum and Natural Gas Lease, you are entering a business deal that could last many years. Make sure you know who you are dealing with.

WHAT ARE YOU GOING TO LEASE?

As indicated in Chapter 2, know what rights you have; do you have all rights or are there exceptions? If you believe you know what rights you own, you can verify your understanding with the company that approaches you, as it should also have done its homework.

In the past, a landowner would typically lease all of their rights to one company. Think about whether you want to follow that form of leasing. If you are in the enviable position of having two companies approach you to lease your land and you have knowledge that one company focuses on drilling deeper formations and the other on shallower targets, you might want to consider leasing certain rights to each company. Think about the layer cake again; one company gets a lease for the bottom half of the cake and the other company gets a lease for the top half. While this may be a little more complicated and require a little more record-keeping on your part, it may allow you to get more value from your land.

Companies may be reluctant to lease the deep rights only, as most like to be able to explore a shallower horizon if their deeper formation does not have oil or gas. What this means is if their first, deeper target is not successful, they would like the option to check out other shallower horizons as they come up the hole. Sometimes companies refer to these as bailout zones. This is especially important to companies if there is a high level of technical risk in the deep formation they are chasing but it is located in an area with a much lower risk in shallower formations. If their high-risk deep play is not successful, they still want to have the ability to check out the shallower layers if they have a lease for all rights on the land.

One situation in which you may be able to negotiate a lease for the shallow rights and a lease for the deep rights is if you are approached by two companies at the same time that have different prospective targets. The companies may not want to compete with each other for a mineral lease if they are focused on different target zones.

As a note of interest, it is very common on Crown lands to have different leases for different horizons on the same piece of land. If this is acceptable to companies on Crown lands, it should also be acceptable on freehold lands.

Once you've identified your rights and perhaps thought about what you are going to lease out, you need to know if you own your land outright or whether you have an undivided fractional interest. If you have an undivided interest and you wish to lease your land, and you know the other people who have an undivided interest in the same land, you could contact them to see if they also want to lease their land. It is highly likely that the land broker or company will already have contacted them directly. If they are interested, you may be able to facilitate leases for all parties. Usually this works only if the undivided working interest owners know each other well and are on good terms with each other.

WHERE ARE YOU GOING TO LEASE?

The physical location of the land is an important component of a mineral lease. The legal land description will be located on your title, as will the description of the mineral rights you hold and your interest in the rights. Although it would be unusual to have a subdivision Plan for mineral rights, if that is the case, the Plan, Block, and Lot numbers would also have to be included on the mineral lease. If a company approaches you, they will have searched the title to your land and you can verify that you both have the same information.

WHEN ARE YOU GOING TO GET A LEASE ON YOUR LAND?

If you see wells being drilled around you, you can be proactive (instead of reactive) by contacting the Explorer about leasing your land. You can also just wait until they approach you and react at that time.

As explained in an earlier section, a company considers many factors when determining where to explore. One of the key factors is whether a company believes there is oil and/or gas in your land that can be produced at a profit using existing technology. It is a good idea to understand the "what" and "where" information about your land ownership before you are approached.

WHY WOULD YOU WANT A MINERAL LEASE ON YOUR LAND?

This question was partly answered in the "Explore and Develop Your Land Yourself" section above, which describes what is involved in developing your mineral rights yourself.

Your mineral rights are an asset that potentially has value if there is oil and gas in your land and you can get it developed. If you can get someone to develop it for you without any risk or cost to you, you can realize value from the asset through the royalties you will negotiate through your lease.

If you don't want to develop the asset at this time, there may be some drainage from your land if a well is drilled on adjacent land, depending on the reservoir and the type of rock that the oil and gas is in. In some types of rock, oil and gas can move freely. In other types of rock, oil and gas do not move freely at all and often require some form of special treatment in order to be "released" from the rock so that they can move freely and be captured at the surface.

Think about being on a beach and watching how easily water moves through the sand as the water comes ashore. Now think about holding a piece of coal or a shale tile and how difficult it would be for water to move through it (instead

Figure 11: Simplified view of a reef

Slice down through the earth:

There may be accumulations of oil or gas at the tops of the reefs.

Aerial view looking down over four Sections of land showing the tops of the reefs

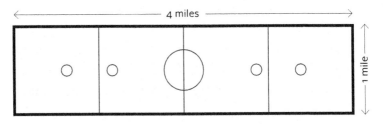

of over it). There is a wide range of rock material holding the various oil and gas resources underground. Sometimes it is like sand, sometimes it is like shale, and sometimes it is some combination of rock types. Whether adjacent drilling will cause drainage from your land depends on the type of rock the oil or gas is being produced from.

In addition, sometimes physical structures deep in the earth determine whether there is drainage on your land. In fact, some of these physical structures may determine if there is oil and/or gas in your land. For example, if companies in the area are producing from structures known as reefs (see Figure 11), there is a good chance that the oil or gas is contained in relatively small pieces of land. Though large reef structures have been found in the past, companies are now finding much smaller reefs.

If wells are being drilled all around your land, you may want to have your land drilled sooner rather than later so you can share in the production from the pool or reservoir that is likely crossing over into your land. Leasing your rights to a company that has the technical expertise, personnel, and finances to find the hydrocarbons, drill for them, and market them will likely be quicker than trying to do these things yourself.

Key Points in This Chapter

- As a mineral landowner, you can choose to sell your land, explore and develop it yourself, lease it to someone else to explore or develop, or do nothing.

- If you decide to enter into a lease to allow a company to explore or develop your mineral rights, do your homework so you know who you are dealing with. While you cannot prevent the original party from assigning the lease to someone else in the future, you can try to enter into a lease with someone that you think will actually drill on your land.

- Be prepared to lease your land by understanding what you have to lease in terms of the rights you own, where the land is located, and how much of the land you own.

6

Key Clauses to Consider When Leasing Your Land

GENERALLY, A LANDOWNER leases their land to an oil and gas company for a certain period in exchange for a bonus consideration (often based on a certain number of dollars per hectare or acre). This gives the company the right to work the land and, if it finds something, to produce from the land, at which point it also pays the landowner a royalty.

The Canadian Association of Petroleum Landmen has developed a number of standard form leases to simplify matters for both companies and landowners. Currently, a couple of standard form leases are commonly in use. Even if a company prefers to use a standard form lease, you can still ask questions about different areas in the form. If the landman you are dealing with does not know the answers to your questions, ask them to find the answers for you. As with any agreement you enter into, make sure you understand what you are agreeing to and what you are signing.

Key Clauses

Generally, a standard form lease has an offer in three key areas: term, bonus consideration, and royalty.

TERM

How long is the primary term of the lease? In other words, how long does the company have to do its initial exploration work and, if it chooses, to drill a well? In the past, five-year lease terms were common. Today, it is very common to see three-year primary terms or even shorter terms of one or two years. Whether a company will agree to a shorter lease term will depend on how much exploratory work and mapping it has done in the area—possibly including your land—and how soon it wants to drill the prospect. As a note of interest, the primary term for a lease on Crown lands is typically five years.

BONUS CONSIDERATION

How much is the company willing to pay for the right to explore on your land? The bonus consideration is usually a dollar figure per hectare/acre multiplied by the number of hectares/acres that you own. While there might be a going rate for the area, the bonus consideration is negotiated between the parties.

My opinion is that landowners should not get too hung up on this number. The real value to the landowner comes when a company has drilled the land, found economic resources, and starts to pay a royalty to the landowner on the production coming from the well or wells on the land.

Depending on the type of resource found, these royalties could last for a very long time.

Note that shorter primary terms will often mean slightly less money for the landowner, because the company does not have as much time to explore and possibly drill the land. To acquire a lease on Crown lands, companies submit sealed bids at regularly scheduled Crown land sales. For leases, the bonus consideration is part of the sealed bid. Some other forms of dispositions may require a work commitment. Further information on Crown land sales is provided in Chapter 7.

ROYALTY

If the exploration is successful and the company drills a well that is capable of production, what percentage of production will the landowner receive? In the past, royalties were often one-eighth of the minerals or a 12.5 percent royalty. More recently, royalties have ranged from 15 to 20 percent. Again, this is a negotiated number between the parties. In almost all cases, the landowner's share of production will be marketed with the company's share of production. After the costs of producing the oil or gas are deducted (assuming this is allowed under the lease; often there is a maximum deduction), the company sends the net proceeds of the royalty to the landowner.

In some resource plays, a mineral landowner may be asked to share the risk of drilling by agreeing to accept a smaller royalty if production levels are lower. This is often referred to as a sliding scale or step royalty. This may allow a company to continue producing a substance even though the production rates are low. Some costs decrease with the lower production while some costs remain the same. A company may want to continue producing a well with low productivity for technical reasons, such as when it is expecting the production rates to increase once the fluids that have been used to treat the formation have been returned to the surface. It is sometimes better to keep producing those wells, and the economics may allow the company to do so if there is a lower royalty rate on lower production levels. Once the production increases, the landowner will share in the increased production with a higher royalty rate.

While as a landowner you would, of course, like a higher royalty, you need to understand that the company needs to be fairly compensated for taking on the risk and expense of drilling an oil and gas well. If no oil or gas is found, the company gets no returns. You will also not get any royalties, but you will have received the initial bonus consideration. You also have the ability to lease your land again when the rights to it return to you at the end of the lease term. Just because one company did not have success drilling does not mean the land is automatically worthless from an oil and gas perspective. Another company may wish to pursue a different idea or target or they may have new technology that proved successful in other areas.

New technology sometimes helps the industry to "see" a little more clearly what might be below us in the earth's layers. For example, improvements in computer technology have increased the amount of data that can be processed in a shorter period of time. Improvements in how increased amounts of data can be manipulated can help technical people visualize prospects in three dimensions rather than two. New technology may also allow the recovery of oil or gas where it could not be recovered before, or it can help to enhance the recovery so that more resources can be recovered with fewer wells. For example, companies are now producing natural gas from coals, whereas in the early 1990s, this was unsuccessful. Another example is the increase in horizontal wells to produce oil and natural gas from shales. Besides developing new technologies to drill very long, horizontal wells, techniques to complete these wells, including fracking, are contributing to higher gas production in North America and elsewhere.

Gross Royalty Trusts and Other Royalties

Sometimes titles contain a caveat that refers to a Gross Royalty Trust (GRT) Agreement. This is a type of agreement put in place by trust companies in the early 1950s. Trust companies approached landowners to assign any royalties coming from their land to the trust company in exchange for certificates representing units in the trust. Only the royalty was assigned; the landowner kept the bonus consideration and any rentals paid. Once a GRT was set up and registered on the title, the royalty for any producing well was paid to the trust company. After keeping an administration fee, the trust company would send out the remaining royalty amount to the GRT certificate holders; the amount each certificate holder received depended on how many units they held.

GRT certificates were easy to transfer until about 1957, and many landowners used the certificates as a form of estate planning by giving them to their immediate family and other relatives. Others sold the certificates to third parties, which allowed them to get immediate value from their land without having to sell it or wait for a successful well to be drilled. The individuals or companies that held these GRT certificates held a share of the royalties on the land through the GRT Agreement.

I have seen various forms of GRT Agreement over the years naming various trust companies as the trustee. Computershare Trust Company of Canada is the successor to most of the original trust companies that entered into this type of agreement.

A common form of GRT Agreement splits a 12.5 percent royalty into 500 units. GRT certificates were issued stating how many units an individual or company had and how many units were issued in total. In this example, one unit was entitled to 1/500 of the 12.5 percent royalty, which translates into a royalty of 0.025 percent.

A GRT Agreement was registered as a caveat on the title when the landowner signed the agreement. The mineral rights could have been sold or willed to other individuals thereafter, but the GRT likely remained an encumbrance on the title.

Let's say that you are a mineral landowner and you have recently signed a Petroleum and Natural Gas Lease that will pay you a royalty of 15 percent on any production coming from the land, and there is a GRT Agreement registered against your land. Because of this prior agreement, the trust company may be entitled to the first 12.5 percent of the royalty and the remaining 2.5 percent of the royalty would belong to you as the Lessor. This is probably okay with you if the GRT certificates are held by your family (near and distant relatives) and possibly by some of your neighbours (past and present). It may not be okay if you did not know that this GRT Agreement existed or, if you did know about it, you did not understand how it would impact your mineral rights.

The company that has drilled the well that is now on production may elect to pay you, the Lessor, the full 15 percent; you would then be responsible for remitting the 12.5 percent to the trust company. The company owning the well could also elect to pay the trust company its 12.5 percent royalty and you the 2.5 percent royalty. How a company chooses to handle this depends on many different factors, but two key considerations are the wording of the GRT Agreement and the wording of the lease agreement that it has with you.

Within the past twenty years, some GRT Agreements have been legally challenged as to whether they are still in effect on the relevant lands, and some cases have gone before the courts. My understanding is that the central issue in these legal challenges is whether the GRT Agreement on a particular piece of land created a continuing interest in that land, or whether it was simply a contractual interest between the trust company and the original landowner who signed the trust agreement. Since it is critical to know the wording of the GRT Agreement and how it was set up, I cannot speculate on whether a particular GRT Agreement is valid or not. For landowners who would like to check on the validity of a particular GRT Agreement, I suggest you start by contacting Computershare Trust Company of Canada. While it may be necessary later in your investigations to hire a lawyer, Computershare has seen many types of GRT Agreements and has a good sense as to which ones remain valid.

I have also seen other forms of agreements caveated on a title that assign a royalty to an individual or company other than a trust company. In many of these cases, the royalty is small, such as 1 percent. Also in many of these cases, we don't know the history of why the royalty was assigned, we just know that it is on the title, and we may have even been able to get a copy of the agreement from the party claiming the interest in the royalty. Again, depending on the wording in the Petroleum and Natural Gas Lease you have signed with a company, that company may choose to pay the royalty to you and expect you to forward the 1 percent royalty to its rightful owner, or they may choose to pay the 1 percent royalty owner directly.

Other Important Clauses

In this section, I will discuss some of the other important clauses in most freehold mineral leases that a mineral landowner should be aware of and understand. I will discuss only the general principles, because the actual clauses will be specific to a particular lease. Be sure to read your lease to see what clauses apply in your particular case and the specific wording of the clauses.

DELAY RENTAL PAYMENT

You will recall that the term of a lease is usually three to five years. Most leases provide for an annual payment that the Lessee (the company) makes to the Lessor (the landowner) if they have not drilled a well in the year leading up to the anniversary date of the lease. The delay rental payment allows the Lessee to delay the drilling of a well for an additional year.

SHUT-IN ROYALTY

Most leases contain a clause that provides for a yearly payment that the Lessee makes to the Lessor in the event that the company has drilled a well on the lands but the well is shut in or not producing. This annual payment is made on the anniversary date of the lease.

There could be many reasons for a well to be shut in. If a well that has been producing in the past is currently not producing, it may need some maintenance work, or the original formation may have depleted, or it may no longer be economic to produce the well at current prices. The company is likely trying to determine its next steps.

If a well has been drilled on the land but has never produced, the Lessee would make a shut-in payment to the Lessor on the anniversary date to continue the lease for another year. One reason the well may not be producing is that there are no pipelines close enough to place the well on production. Taking into account the cost of building the pipeline and the expected production from the well, the company may not consider it economic to connect the well at this time. The company may be waiting until more wells are drilled in the area so that the cost of the pipeline can be shared by all the wells, or it may be waiting for prices to increase.

OFFSET WELL

The offset well clause provides a mechanism whereby landowners can protect themselves from drainage if a well is drilled on a DSU beside their land (the offset section). Offsets can be on the adjacent DSU (lateral offset) or a DSU where the corner touches a corner of your land (diagonal offset; see Figure 12). In some cases, both situations could exist at the same time.

It is very important to understand how your lease defines an offset. For example, at a minimum, an offset usually includes laterally adjoining DSUs. However, the offset definition in your lease may include both laterally and diagonally adjoining DSUs. An offset well is typically a well that has been drilled after the date of your lease and is producing from a specific horizon that is also contained in your lease. If you have a producing well on your land, the offset well will be producing from a different horizon.

Once an offset well has been drilled, generally a period starts in which the Lessee can choose one of several options. Sometimes the Lessor needs to serve a notice to the Lessee to start the clock. I must emphasize that you need to look at

Figure 12A: Lateral offsets

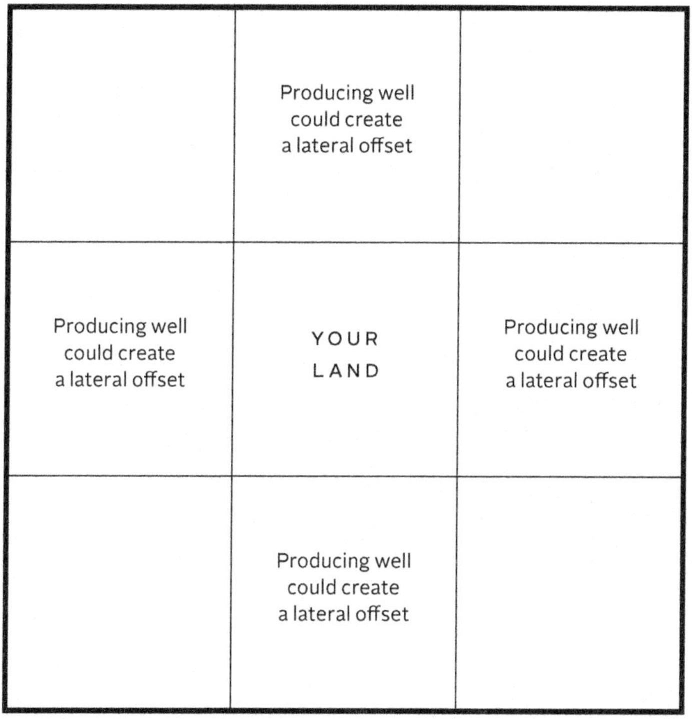

	Producing well could create a lateral offset	
Producing well could create a lateral offset	YOUR LAND	Producing well could create a lateral offset
	Producing well could create a lateral offset	

Each square represents a drilling spacing unit

Check your lease to see if lateral offsets are included in the definition of offset wells in your particular situation.

---

your particular lease to see what the clause says and what the options are, but the three most common are for the Lessee to:

- Drill a well to the same horizon as the offset well
- Surrender the zone or rights (a choice in some leases)
- Pay a compensatory royalty (discussed in more depth below)

Figure 12B: Diagonal offsets

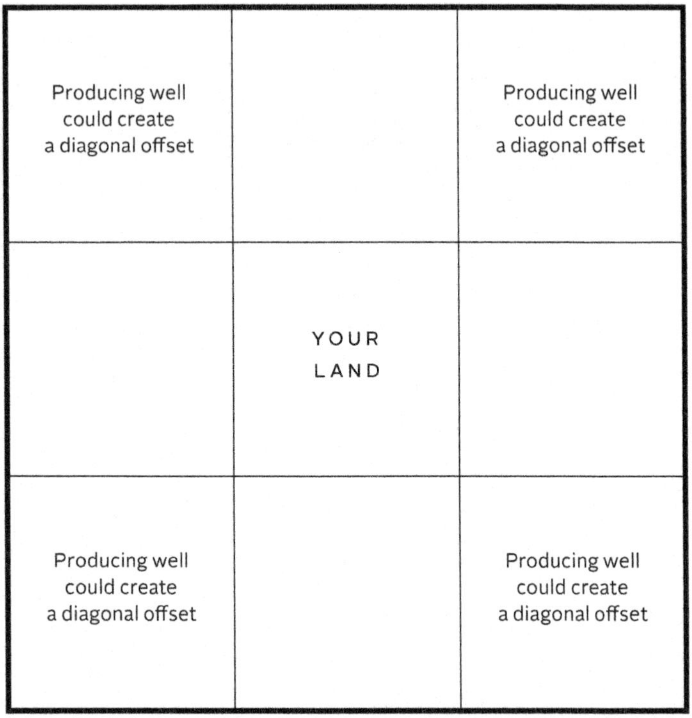

Producing well could create a diagonal offset		Producing well could create a diagonal offset
	YOUR LAND	
Producing well could create a diagonal offset		Producing well could create a diagonal offset

Each square represents a drilling spacing unit

Check your lease to see if diagonal offsets are included in the definition of offset wells in your particular situation.

Until about the late 1990s or early 2000s, most of the exploration, drilling, and production in western Canada were out of what is known as conventional resources. Think back to the beach scene and remember how easily water and air flow through sand. Other than the oilsands, which require specialized processes, these conventional resources made up the bulk of production in western Canada.

As technology developed and improved—and continues to do so—there has been more activity in what are typically known as unconventional resources. These are the resources found in formations such as coals, shales, and tight sands. In our layer cake analogy, some layers of the cake are like a light sponge cake (conventional resources), while other layers are like a dense, heavy chocolate torte layer (unconventional resources).

Offsets make a lot of sense when we are talking about conventional resources. However, they may not be as relevant in unconventional resources, as the oil or gas does not flow through this type of rock as easily. Whether there is drainage in unconventional resources will not be debated in this book, and it is not the landowner's responsibility to know what type of resource the company is exploring for.

It is my opinion that the landowner shares responsibility for identifying when a well has been drilled on offset lands. Yes, the oil and gas industry has access to information, but so do landowners. Educate yourself so that you are in a better position to negotiate a fair lease. Ask questions so that you fully understand the contract you are entering into. If the company you are negotiating with is not willing to answer your questions, you may want to reconsider doing business with that company. A fair amount of information is available on various websites, but consider whether the source of the information you find online can be trusted. The websites listed at the end of this book are good places to start your research. This involves some work on the part of the landowner, but it is your asset. If the land were my asset, I'd want to learn as much as I could about it.

If the company's corporate strategy is to pursue natural gas in shallow formations and the offset well is in a deeper oil formation, the offset may not even be on the company's radar. If you know about the offset well, bring it to the company's attention. At the very least, this may speed up the company's payment of compensatory royalties, or you may get the land rights back so you can lease them to someone else. The land is your asset; know what's happening around it.

SURRENDER

In an offset situation, a common option for a Lessee is to surrender the rights that the offset well is producing from back to you, the Lessor. You would then be in a position to lease those rights to another party. Perhaps you could contact other companies in the area or even the company that has drilled the offset well to see if they are interested in leasing the rights from you.

The Lessee can choose to surrender the lease back to the Lessor at any time. Their rights and obligations remain in effect until the date of surrender.

COMPENSATORY ROYALTY

Another common option a Lessee has under an offset situation is to pay a compensatory royalty. The royalty a Lessee pays to a Lessor is based on what is being produced in the offset wells. The concept of a compensatory royalty is to pay you, the Lessor, a royalty as if you had a well drilled to the same formation on your lands.

Check your lease to confirm how the calculation is made. If there is one offset well, the calculation is relatively simple.

The production from that well along with the royalty rate on your lease will be used to calculate the compensatory royalty. If there is more than one offset well, typically an average is taken of all the production rates from the offset wells. That average production rate is then multiplied by the royalty rate on your lease to determine the compensatory royalty to be paid that month.

I have seen many different ways to calculate a compensatory royalty, so it is important to check the wording on your lease to see what applies in your case.

DEEP RIGHTS REVERSION

This is a relatively new concept in freehold mineral leases, but the Government of Alberta has had this in place since the early 1980s on new Crown leases. The concept is that during the primary term of the lease, the company has the right to drill a well to "win, take, or remove" petroleum substances. At the end of the primary term, the company can continue the lease, but only down to the base of the formations they have proven are productive.

Typically, if a company is producing from a certain formation, it will continue to hold the rights down to the base of that producing formation. The rights below that revert back to the landowner, who can then try to lease the deep rights to another company. With luck, the other company may be able to develop those rights.

Leases that have this provision will have a deep rights reversion clause. This takes a little more effort on the part of the landowner, as you need to start thinking of your land in three dimensions and perhaps familiarize yourself with some of the more common formations producing oil and gas in the area where your land is located. The potential reward for this extra effort is that you may be able to fully develop your land from top to bottom (assuming there are petroleum substances to be found on your land that can be explored and developed economically).

Questions to Ask in the Leasing Process

The following is a short list of questions you may want to ask when considering or negotiating a lease. Some of the questions are for the company wanting to lease your land, and some are questions you will want to ask yourself to make sure you understand the various pieces of a very complex picture. The company representative or broker may not have or want to provide all the answers, but you can still ask the questions. In no way is this list meant to be exhaustive. If you are curious about something not mentioned here, I encourage you to ask the question.

- What is the company exploring for? Oil or gas? Shallow or deep?
  This may help you decide whom to lease to, particularly if more than one company is after your land. Leasing shallow rights to a company chasing shallow gas and the balance of the lands to another company will help to maximize the possible returns on your land.

- Is the company ready to drill?
  This may help you determine the length of the primary term.

You may also discover if the company has leased the rest of the DSU.

- Are there pipelines nearby? If the company finds oil or gas, how long will it take to get it on production?

  The company may or may not be able to answer this, but its response may tell you how far along it is in the exploration process.

- What are the conditions under which a lease will continue past its primary term?

  This may not be a question for the company you are talking to, but you do want to have an answer to this in your own mind as you are negotiating, as it will tell you what the company needs to do to continue the lease past its initial expiry date. It also tells you when your land rights could return to you if the company doesn't do any work on your land. When the rights return, you can lease them out again.

- Will a deep rights reversion clause appear in the lease?

  This may allow some rights below the company's zone of production to return to you at the end of the initial term. You can then try to lease the deep rights to another company.

- What happens when wells are drilled that offset my land?

  See the section in this chapter about offset well clauses.

- If I have only a small interest in the land, has the company been able to locate all other landowners?

  If the company has not located everyone, ask if it will share the names of the people it is seeking; perhaps you can help

track down a long-lost cousin or some other member of your family. Remember that a company cannot apply for a licence to drill until it can show regulators that it has control over the DSU. It is in your best interest if all parties owning an interest in the land can be located.

Pre-Lease Agreements

Sometimes the company is unable to enter into a lease right away. However, if it is interested in your land, it may want to enter into an agreement that could lead to a lease, such as an Option to Lease or an Agreement to Acquire, otherwise known as a top lease.

OPTION TO LEASE

Sometimes a company will take an Option to Lease, particularly in an area that has complex or fragmented ownership. The option gives the company time to determine whether it will be able to acquire all lands in the DSU. The term of the option depends on what is negotiated between the parties, but terms of three, six, or twelve months are common. The landowner (Optionor) is paid a consideration for the option by the company (Optionee). If the option is exercised, a lease comes into effect and the bonus consideration for the lease is paid. Parties negotiate the terms and conditions of the lease at the same time that they negotiate the option. The lease containing all the agreed-to terms is usually attached to the Option to Lease document.

In an Option to Lease agreement, the Optionee decides

if it is going to exercise the option. If the Optionee decides not to exercise the option within the time allowed in the agreement, the option will terminate and the landowner or Optionor is free to negotiate a land deal with someone else.

AGREEMENT TO ACQUIRE

Sometimes a company will pay the landowner to enter into an Agreement to Acquire instead of an option. In this case, a lease will automatically come into effect as of a certain date or when a certain event occurs. The most common event is when the land is already under an existing lease and that lease expires due to no activity on the land; in this case, the lease attached to an Agreement to Acquire would come into effect and the company would pay the bonus consideration attached to the new lease. As with an Option to Lease, the parties agree to the terms of the new lease—such as bonus consideration, term, and royalty—during the negotiations for the Agreement to Acquire.

It is not always clear to other companies when an existing lease is terminated; all they know is whether a caveat has been filed on the landowner's title. Therefore, landowners need to know when they are free to enter into an agreement with another party.

Final Thoughts on Leasing

A key point when you are negotiating a lease is to understand all of the terms of your lease before you sign it. It is not enough to ask only about the primary term, initial bonus consideration, and royalty. Having a clear understanding of all other clauses in the lease will clarify the rights and obligations of both parties, which should help minimize future misunderstandings.

The relationship between the parties is actually a partnership in which one party needs to entice the other to drill by offering terms that make it attractive to do so, and the other party takes on the risk of exploring and potentially drilling for oil and/or gas. The best agreement is one in which each party understands and accepts what they have agreed to and each party is in a win position.

The company wins because it has secured the rights to explore for oil and gas, which, if found, it can sell. As the landowner, you also win because you have the opportunity to get some value for your asset in the form of a royalty. You make money from your asset only if the company doing the exploration makes money.

Treat this as any other business transaction, because that is what this is. If you want to get your land developed, you need to be reasonable, or the company could go elsewhere. Most companies have the choice of many different sandboxes to play in. Make sure you have made it attractive to play in yours.

As a mineral landowner, you have the right to do what you wish with your land. If you wish to sell or lease your land, you have an obligation to know what you have and what you can sell or lease. Once you've entered into an agreement, you have an obligation to understand and follow its terms, just as the company does.

Key Points in This Chapter

- Make sure you understand all terms of the lease you are entering into. It is a business contract, and both parties need to understand their rights and obligations.

- The key components that landowners usually focus on are the term, bonus consideration, and royalty.

- If you have a Gross Royalty Trust Agreement for your land, you should confirm that the agreement still applies and what this means for your own rights.

- Other key lease terms that landowners should understand are the delay rental payment, shut-in royalty, offset well, surrender, compensatory royalty, and deep rights reversion clauses.

- If a company is unable to enter into a lease right away, it may want to enter into an Option to Lease or an Agreement to Acquire.

- As a mineral landowner, you are trying to entice a company to play and drill in your sandbox. Be reasonable in your requests. You will not make any money from your land if the company you have leased it to does not make any money from it.

7

The Leasing Process for Lands Owned by the Government

WHILE THIS BOOK is focused on freehold lands, I thought freehold landowners might be interested to know what happens on lands owned by the government. Because Canada was once a colony under a monarch, these are referred to as Crown lands.

Remember that the Crown holds lands for the benefit of all people in the municipality, province, state, or country in which the lands are located. For example, the Alberta Crown holds title to lands on behalf of all citizens of Alberta. Any bonus considerations and royalties paid to the Alberta government are used to pay for goods and services such as roads, hospitals, and health care to benefit Alberta's citizens. When royalties go down due to a decrease in prices or production, the revenue that the provincial government receives from its mineral rights also goes down.

If the mineral title is held by the Crown and the surface rights are held by a freeholder, the company still needs to get a Surface Lease from the surface landowner to drill a well. If it is unable to reach an agreement with the surface landowner (whether because the surface landowner objects to the location or to the compensation offered), drilling and subsequent royalties on that parcel of Crown land will be delayed until an agreement can be achieved and a well drilled.

This chapter will focus on Alberta Crown lands, but most other provinces in Canada have a similar process as described here. The federal government also has a similar process for its large tracts of federal lands (for example, offshore Newfoundland). Each government has legislation in place to manage its mineral rights, and the various acts and regulations can be found on government webpages. Typically, government departments are established to manage Crown lands and the governing legislation.

Crown Land Sales

In Crown land sales, companies are not actually purchasing title to the land. Rather, they are purchasing the right, through a document such as a permit, licence, or lease, to work the land and, depending on the agreement, produce from the land. The rules and regulations associated with each type of title document are contained in various acts and regulations of the government in question.

Crown land sales happen every two weeks in Alberta, every month in British Columbia, and every other month in Saskatchewan. Sales have established dates and time windows when certain activities associated with a sale are in effect. Sale dates are known well in advance, as are dates for requests for postings, when companies may ask the Crown to offer certain lands and rights at a certain sale. Other provinces and the federal government typically hold their land sales less frequently. Sometimes a government will make a call for postings, and a sale will be held only if that government receives sufficient posting requests.

On Crown sale day, sealed bids are submitted to the Crown (electronically in Alberta, by letter in other jurisdictions). The bids are for the total of the bonus consideration, prescribed fee, and prescribed first-year rental. The fee and rental are prescribed by the government in regulations that govern the lands. Bids must be submitted by a certain date and time. The identity of the successful bidder is published by the Crown shortly after the sale, and the bid amount is debited from the company's account that day.

When I started in the industry, there were no such things as electronic funds transfer or electronic bidding. On Crown sale day in Alberta, a company that wished to submit bids needed to perform many steps before it delivered its bid letters. First it had to determine how much it wanted to bid and prepare the bid letters. It then needed to contact its bank to have individual certified cheques prepared for the total amount of each bid it wanted to submit. Someone, usually a Junior Landman or other junior person in the company, would then have to pick up the cheques at the bank and either bring them back to the office to be attached to the corresponding bid letters or attach them to the bid letters while at the bank.

Once the cheques were attached to the right letters, they were placed in individual envelopes labelled with the sale date and parcel number. The bid envelopes were then delivered to the place designated by the Crown before the deadline. Although a junior person was often given this task, this person had to be responsible and understand the importance of deadlines. If they missed the cut-off time for bids by even a minute or two because they had stopped to pick up a coffee, the bid was not accepted.

The day after the sale, the results would be announced through the printing of a document called the Crown Sale Results. The company representative had to pick up this report at the same place they dropped off the company's bids. The person would quickly check the parcels the company had bid on. If the bids were successful, all was well and they would return to the office with the good news. If the bids were unsuccessful, they had to line up to retrieve the cheques from the unsuccessful bids and either return them to the bank or take them back to the office so they could be deposited into the corporate account (remember that these were certified cheques, so the money had already been taken out of the account).

While certified cheques were cumbersome, my understanding is that they became a requirement of the government many, many years ago when certain companies were very successful at bidding for lands but did not have enough money in their accounts to pay for all of their successful bids. The advent of electronic funds transfer has made it easier for the government to ensure it has the funds before the results are announced. Some jurisdictions still require that individual bid letters be submitted but have modified their payment practices to allow electronic payment.

After a Crown Land Sale

After the land sale process is complete, the Crown issues the appropriate title document to the successful bidder. A Petroleum and Natural Gas Lease from the Alberta Crown is for five years, may be for certain rights only, and has a sliding scale royalty prescribed by the regulations (see Figure 13 for a comparison of freehold and Crown leases). A sliding scale means that as production increases, the royalty rate increases (to a maximum rate).

Figure 13: Freehold Leases Compared to Crown Leases

KEY LEASE COMPONENTS	FREEHOLD LEASE	CROWN LEASE
Term	Three to five years (could be one to two years).	Five years.
Bonus consideration	Negotiated. Generally based on certain amount per acre or hectare.	Sealed bid at regularly scheduled Crown land sales. Results published shortly after sale closes.
Royalty	Negotiated. Could be in range of 15 to 20 percent. Some evolving to step or sliding scale royalty that depends on production rate.	Sliding scale royalty depends on production rate.

As a landowner, you should keep Crown land sales in mind when trying to entice a company to take a lease on your lands. You are competing not only with other landowners when trying to attract a company, but also with the Crown.

Key Points in This Chapter

- Companies acquire leases on Crown lands through a sealed bid process at regularly scheduled Crown land sales.

- Governments manage Crown lands on behalf of and for the benefit of the people within their jurisdictions.

- Companies can lease land for exploration from freeholders or the government.

After Your Land Has Been Leased

Potential Reasons for a Delay in Drilling on Your Land

ONCE A LEASE has been signed, many landowners expect a company to start drilling on their land, and they may get concerned if this doesn't happen right away. Remember that the company (the Lessee) may drill on the land at any point during the primary term of the lease. In signing a lease, the Lessee has the right to drill a well but not necessarily the obligation to do so. A company may delay the drilling of a well for many reasons, some of which are discussed below.

Additional technical work may be required from a geological or geophysical perspective. On some plays, it is very important to identify the target of the well and then develop a drilling plan so that the target can be hit with the drilling bit. The company is trying to hit a target (sometimes a small one) that could be 1,000 to 3,000 metres (3,300 to 10,000 feet) or more below the surface, so a lot of planning is required.

If another company is drilling a well in the area to the same formation, the company with a lease on your land may want to wait until it can get some information from that well before drilling on your land. The additional information might either validate or condemn the geologist's ideas. If there has been no other well drilled to that formation within an area prescribed by the regulations, the other company will sometimes hold its well information confidential for up to a year. If that well information is held "tight," this could delay the drilling of a well on your land until the information is released.

As we learned earlier, a company needs to have control over the complete DSU to apply for a well licence. In Alberta, this is one Section (256 hectares/640 acres) for a gas well and a quarter Section (64 hectares/160 acres) for an oil well. If there are a number of landowners to contact, negotiations can take a long time, as an agreement needs to be reached with each title holder or group of title holders. This also assumes that all title holders can be found, and that is not always the case. As discussed earlier, the company could then apply to the regulator for a compulsory Pooling Order and the Public Trustee would be designated to hold any revenues in trust for the missing title holder.

While negotiations are going on with the mineral landholders, the company will decide when it wishes to approach the surface landowner for a Surface Lease. These negotiations can also be lengthy. If the surface landowner does not object to the location of the well but wants more money for the Surface Lease, there are mechanisms in place for a company to immediately access the land, with a compensation hearing held at a future date.

If the negotiations for the mineral rights and/or surface rights have taken a long time, the economics of drilling the well may have changed. Perhaps the price to be received for the product, be it oil or gas, has gone down. Perhaps the cost of drilling the well has gone up due to the supply and demand for oilfield services and equipment. This may delay the drilling of the well until conditions improve.

Whether there has been a change in the geological view of the lands, a change in the economics, or a shift in the company's focus to another product (gas to oil or vice versa), the company may decide to spend its exploration and drilling dollars elsewhere. Like individuals, corporations tend to have many different areas in which they can spend their money. They owe it to their shareholders to spend their money in the areas and on the prospects where they have the best chance to make the most return.

What Happens if a Company Chooses Not to Drill?

For whatever reason, if the company decides not to drill on your land, it has some choices. It can surrender the lease, allow the lease on your land to expire at the end of the primary term, or try to find another company to drill the land.

It is unlikely that the company will surrender the lease, as it did pay a bonus consideration to acquire it. Also, as quickly as conditions changed to cause the company to delay drilling your land, they could become favourable again. Prices for the commodity could go up and that particular prospect could be in favour once more.

If the company finds another firm to drill on the land, a contract will be negotiated between the two companies. You will likely receive notice that your lease has been assigned to the new company, particularly if the lease has been sold. Occasionally, the first indication that a new company is involved is a new name on the well sign. If you do not live in the area and therefore don't see the well sign or the activity on your land, sometimes your first indication of a change in the Lessee will come when you receive a delay rental, shut-in royalty, or royalty cheque from a different company than the one you signed a lease with.

Company to Company Negotiations

The mineral landowner and other readers of this book may find it interesting to read about some of the types of agreements that a company might enter into with other companies to explore a piece of land. Agreements within the industry use a lot of jargon, and my experience is that a lot of people who work in another part of the industry (for example, engineering, accounting, gas marketing, drilling, or field operations) do not understand the basics of the various agreements that exist between their company and other companies.

The type of deal struck between companies will depend on the stage of exploration or development of the prospect.

As with a mineral lease between a landowner and a company, companies negotiate the terms under which a piece of land will be explored and developed. Presently, I believe that one main difference between the negotiations that occur between a landowner and a company and the negotiations that occur between companies is the knowledge level of the parties. My hope is that this book will serve to increase the knowledge level of the landowner so that the negotiations can occur on a more equal level.

Any number of clauses can be negotiated into company to company agreements, and the results can be very simple or incredibly complex. Depending on the particular circumstances, the concepts in a couple of simple agreements can sometimes be combined so that a more complex agreement evolves. Other times, the landman is challenged to come up with a unique solution to a unique situation. If he or she is able to convince the other company that the solution presented is well thought out and will benefit both companies, the next challenge may be to convince his or her own management team that it is a good solution. Whether I am teaching students at the university or mentoring landmen in the industry, I often say that their toughest negotiations may be with the people in their own companies. Negotiations across the table with another company may be very simple in comparison.

Keep in mind that anything can be negotiated between companies provided that both are in agreement. My experience is that the best negotiations result in an agreement that is a win-win for all parties—i.e., all parties believe they have gained by entering into that agreement. This is particularly important in the Canadian industry due to the relationships that develop among the relatively small number of people (generally landmen) who negotiate land deals on behalf of their companies. If an individual feels that they or their company were "taken" in a deal, the chances of doing a deal with that same company or landman again in the future are very slim.

The other thing I tell the students I instruct or the landmen I mentor is to maintain their integrity, as it is the one thing they have control of in this industry. If they plan to have a long and successful career, their reputation is critical to their success. Other important elements are the relationships they develop during their career and how they manage and cultivate those relationships. It's not just about how many business cards are in one's Rolodex (I know I'm dating myself here). It's about learning who those individuals are and what's important to them in their daily lives.

I recall having a conversation with a counterpart in the United States about a particular clause in an agreement. He asked what I would do if the other company violated the terms of the agreement. I told him that I would probably call up that company's landman and invite him for coffee or lunch to try to sort it out. His response was that "you Canadians are so damn civil up there."

I explained to him that (at the time) the Canadian Association of Petroleum Landmen had about 1,600 members. Most of these members worked as mineral landmen, and about 95 percent worked within a ten-block by ten-block area in downtown Calgary. Contrast that to the American Association of Professional Landmen, which had approximately 16,000 members. While there are certainly concentrations of landmen in Texas, Oklahoma, and Louisiana, and I have met many landmen from those states, I have also met landmen who live and work in New York State, Colorado, Wyoming, Montana, Alaska, California, and New Mexico. Since landmen in Canada work in a much more concentrated area than landmen in the United States, we need to make sure we spend a lot of time nurturing our relationships in the industry, since these relationships contribute to our personal success and the success of the companies we work for.

The following is a brief overview of some of the basic agreements that may be negotiated between companies. The summaries include a basic description of terms and why companies might enter into that form of agreement.

JOINT OPERATING AGREEMENT

Companies typically enter into this first basic agreement when they have jointly acquired some land and want to explore and develop it together. As a simple example, let's say that Company A and Company B each bore 50 percent of the costs to acquire some land and they wish to explore it on a 50:50 basis.

Why would companies want to enter into this type of agreement in this highly competitive industry? There are a few possibilities. Sometimes the geologists in the two companies know each other and have shared information or received the same information from a third-party data supplier. Because each company has the same information, they may decide to put their resources together to acquire the land rather than compete with each other. This form of cooperation may allow them to acquire twice as much land than they would have had they gone it alone. The other possibility is that they can acquire a lease on the same amount of land by each paying half of what they would have paid had they each acquired 100 percent. By cooperating, they have been able to acquire the land with a reduced net cost. Going by itself, a company may not have been successful in acquiring all of the land it wanted to acquire.

If the prospect is particularly risky because it is a new concept or a new sandbox, a company may want to share the risk with another company that has a similar idea. This allows both companies to still test the concept but share the risk and reduce the amount of capital required, thereby freeing up money for other pursuits.

The Canadian Association of Petroleum Landmen has developed over time various versions of a standard Operating Procedure that can be attached to the main agreement listing the companies and their interests. The Operating Procedure describes items such as how the land will be managed, including which of the parties will be Operator; how notices of proposed operations will work; what happens if a party does not want to participate in a proposed operation; what happens if one party wants to sell its interest; and a number of other situations that could arise with respect to the land. The Petroleum Accountants Society of Canada has developed over time various versions of an Accounting

Procedure that sets out the rates and elections that can apply to the property and includes such items as the overhead rate the Operator can charge the other parties, the operating advances that can be requested, how field offices and employees will be charged out, and the timing for payment of invoices.

The Joint Operating Agreement can cover a single Section of land or many Sections. It can be a two-party agreement or it can have multiple parties, some with large working interests and some with small working interests.

POOLING AGREEMENT

We discussed earlier in this book that a company needs to try to acquire all of the land in a DSU to apply for a well licence. Sometimes a company is able to secure only part of the DSU while another company (or companies) leases other parts from other landowners. What's a company that wants to drill on the lands to do in this situation?

The answer is that it negotiates a Pooling Agreement with the other companies that hold the leases making up the rest of the DSU. It can of course pool more lands than a single DSU, and it may want to do this to share the costs and risks of exploring a particular prospect. Once a Pooling Agreement is in effect, typically an Operating Procedure and an Accounting Procedure like the ones described in the previous section are attached as schedules to the agreement to govern the actions among the pooled parties.

Usually a Pooling Agreement assumes there are Petroleum and Natural Gas Leases covering all lands that are to be pooled. The companies that hold these leases (Lessees) will be the named parties to the Pooling Agreement. If a landowner has not signed a lease with anyone, there are likely some reasons for that. If this landowner's land is the only piece that has not been leased (particularly if it is a small piece), one of the companies (usually the Operator) can apply to the regulator for a compulsory Pooling Order; this was described in Chapter 3.

The leases being pooled can be non-cross conveyed or cross conveyed. Under the more common non-cross conveyed pooling, each company contributing a lease to the pooling retains its underlying ownership and is responsible for its own lease. That is, they are responsible for paying all rentals and royalties owing to their Lessors and generally to keep their leases in good standing. Under a cross conveyed pooling, there is a transfer of ownership and one company will be designated as the party responsible for paying all amounts on all leases. This company is usually designated as the Operator of the pooled lands under the Operating Procedure attached to the Pooling Agreement.

The lands are usually pooled on an acreage basis so that the resulting pooled interest of each party depends on how much land each company contributed. A simple case would be where a company holds a 100 percent interest in half of the land contributed to the pooling and another company holds a 100 percent interest in the other half of the contributed land. This would result in each company holding a 50 percent interest in all of the land contributed to the pooling.

In the more complicated example shown in Figure 14, it is simple to calculate Company A's and Company D's interests,

Figure 14: Pooling example

Pooling one Section of mineral land rights on an acreage basis

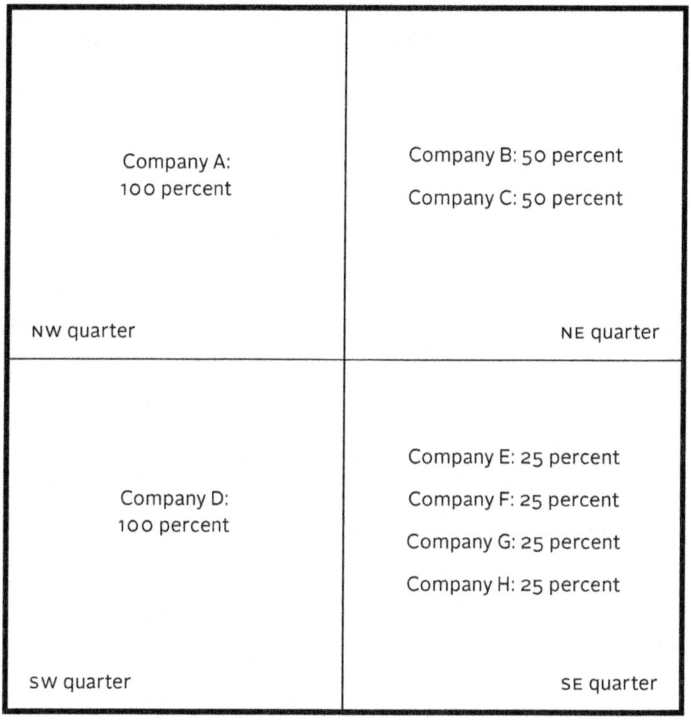

Company A: 100 percent NW quarter	Company B: 50 percent Company C: 50 percent NE quarter
Company D: 100 percent SW quarter	Company E: 25 percent Company F: 25 percent Company G: 25 percent Company H: 25 percent SE quarter

Resulting pooled interests

Company A	25 percent	Company E	6.25 percent
Company B	12.5 percent	Company F	6.25 percent
Company C	12.5 percent	Company G	6.25 percent
Company D	25 percent	Company H	6.25 percent

as they have each contributed a quarter Section or 25 percent to the pooled lands. Companies B and C each have a 50 percent interest in a quarter Section, so they each have contributed 12.5 percent (50 percent of 25 percent) to the pooling.

Companies E, F, G, and H each have a 25 percent interest in a quarter Section, so they each have contributed 6.25 percent (25 percent of 25 percent) to the pooling. The resulting pooled interests of the companies are shown in Figure 14.

FARM-OUT OR FARM-IN AGREEMENT

As mentioned above, after acquiring land, a company may choose not to explore on it for any variety of reasons. Since the company has already paid a bonus consideration to acquire the land, it may not want to surrender it. Instead, it will likely try to find another company to explore on the land. The company that holds the land is referred to as the Farmor and the company that will be doing the work is referred to as the Farmee.

The name of the actual agreement depends on which side of the deal a company is on. The Farmor refers to this type of agreement as a Farm-out Agreement, as it is going to farm out the land it holds to another company to do the work. The Farmee may refer to this same agreement as a Farm-in Agreement, as it is going to farm in into land held by another company and do work on it.

So the Farmor contributes land to the deal and the Farmee contributes money to explore on the land. What does the Farmee get for doing the work? There is no standard answer to this question, as many variations of agreement can be negotiated between the parties. Since companies are not required to disclose the terms of these private agreements, we never actually know all the terms. However, I can share some of the more common terms I have seen:

- Farmee to pay 100 percent of the costs of drilling, completing, and equipping a well to earn 100 percent of the proceeds from production of that well until it has recovered all of its costs. At that time (typically known in the industry as "payout"), the Farmee's interest would drop to 50 percent and the Farmor comes back in for a 50 percent interest. At that point, 50 percent of the land would be held by the Farmor and 50 percent by the Farmee, and all revenues and expenses would be shared on that basis. Before payout occurs, the Farmor would get a gross overriding royalty of a negotiated percentage of production (gross or net of costs, depending on what is negotiated). This negotiated percentage is typically between 5 and 15 percent, and it can be a flat royalty or a sliding scale royalty that increases (to a maximum) as production increases. Typically it is a flat royalty if the Farmee is producing gas and a sliding scale royalty if the Farmee is producing oil.

- Farmee to pay 100 percent of the costs of drilling, completing, and equipping a well to earn a 100 percent working interest in the land. Upon the Farmee earning its working interest in the land, the Farmor reserves a non-convertible gross overriding royalty. In this case, the Farmor continues to receive a royalty even if the Farmee has recovered all of its costs. The Farmee continues to be responsible for 100 percent of the expenses and receives 100 percent of the revenue less the royalty it has to pay to the Farmor and the Lessor (the landowner who originally leased the land to the Farmor).

- Farmee to pay 100 percent of the costs of drilling, completing, and equipping a well to earn a 50 percent working interest in the land. In this case, the Farmee has no opportunity to recover its costs before it is in a 50 percent working interest. Sometimes, to make this attractive to the Farmee, the Farmor will allow more land to be earned by the Farmee for doing the work.

As you can see, many variations can arise out of this type of agreement, since any part of the agreement can be negotiated. The Canadian Association of Petroleum Landmen has developed various forms of agreements that can be used in negotiating farm-out situations. While these forms have been of great assistance, the landman should still know what agreements are needed depending on the situation and what they negotiate.

In the examples above, I've used 100 percent and 50 percent working interests for simplicity. These interests can vary depending on the skill of the people involved in the negotiations. I've often encouraged students and younger landmen to think outside the box. While standard terms and agreements may work, sometimes there is a better solution if a landman can apply a little creative thinking to the situation. This tends to involve more work and take more time to negotiate a deal, but if it brings more value to both parties, it's worth it.

SEISMIC OPTION AGREEMENT

Similar to a Farm-out Agreement, in a Seismic Option Agreement the Optionor is the company holding the land and the

Optionee is the company willing to spend money to explore the land. Sometimes further information is required before a company is prepared to commit money to drilling a well. Perhaps the geologist is trying to get a better picture of what the structures look like deep down in the earth's layers, and he or she may ask for help from another type of earth scientist known as a geophysicist.

The area of geophysics most commonly used in the search for oil and gas is seismology, which is essentially a study of waves and how they travel through the earth. Many people are familiar with the waves that occur when the tide is coming in or going out. Fewer people are familiar with the waves that occur when an earthquake hits a region and causes waves on the surface of the earth or water (sometimes resulting in tsunamis).

Even fewer people are aware of the waves that occur when an energy source at the surface of the earth creates a vibration that then travels down through the various layers of the earth; this is what seismologists study. The different compositions of the various layers in the earth will allow these waves of energy to either pass through a particular layer or bounce off the layer. The different compositions of the layers also affect the speed of these waves. The energy reflected back to the surface is recorded, and using various mathematical formulas and computer programs, a geophysicist generates a picture of what the layers below the surface might look like. A seismic program would consist of a number of energy discharges and multiple receivers to record the energy being returned to the surface. Different types

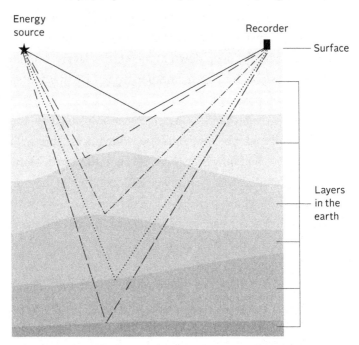

Figure 15: Simplified view of what happens during one piece (or one shot) of a seismic program

This diagram shows one energy source and one recorder or receiver, known as a geophone. However, there are actually multiple recorders for each energy source. A seismic program would have multiple energy sources. The result: a lot of data that can be processed and manipulated by computers.

---

of energy sources are used, but traditionally, small shots of dynamite are placed in small holes drilled into the ground—hence the industry phrase of "shooting" a seismic program. Figure 15 shows a simple picture of what happens when seismic is shot in an area.

If the Optionee needs additional seismic information to enhance the picture it sees below the earth's surface before committing to drilling a well, it will sometimes commit to shooting a seismic program consisting of a certain number of kilometres or miles of seismic by a certain date. Time will then be built into the agreement to process and interpret the data. At another agreed-to date, the Optionee will have to decide whether it wants to drill a well. If it elects to drill, the agreement now looks very much like a Farm-out Agreement, with all the different earning possibilities discussed above.

If the Optionee elects not to drill, the land returns to the Optionor, and the Optionor will receive a copy of the seismic data. The Optionor is then free to try to entice someone else to drill on the land.

JOINT VENTURE AGREEMENT

Sometimes the agreements that are negotiated cover very large areas, contain commitments to drill a large number of wells, or involve large dollar amounts. Typically, when the scope of a project is very large, the agreements that companies enter into are referred to as Joint Venture Agreements. The agreements described above could be viewed as specific forms of Joint Venture Agreements.

As with negotiations between landowners and companies, negotiations between companies can result in different agreements. The main difference in these negotiating scenarios is the knowledge level of the negotiating parties; company representatives, often landmen, tend to have a similar knowledge base to start their negotiations, but their different skill levels will lead to different results.

The skill of a company's negotiator in reaching agreements with other companies is only one of many factors that determine whether a company is successful. Other factors include whether the geological interpretation is solid, whether wells can be drilled and completed effectively and cost-efficiently, whether the wells can be operated in a cost-effective manner, and whether overhead costs can be kept at a reasonable level. However, skilled negotiators go a long way toward ensuring that successful agreements can and will continue to be negotiated.

What Happens Next if a Company Drills a Well on Your Land?

If a company does drill on your land during the primary term of your lease and finds something it can physically and economically produce, you may not receive your royalties right away. If the product is natural gas, it doesn't really have a value until the company can get it to a market and sell it. A pipeline needs to be built so that the gas can be taken off your land and transported to a larger pipeline through which it can flow into a central facility for processing and/or compression. Often the natural gas that comes from a well contains other things besides methane gas. Sometimes impurities (such as water) or other gases or products (such as hydrogen sulphide or nitrogen) are mixed in with the methane and need to be removed. Once the product has been treated, it can then be moved into a sales line.

Things are a little simpler if the product is oil, in that a pipeline isn't always necessary to initially produce the well.

Oil can be stored in tanks on-site on the Surface Lease until there is sufficient volume to truck it off-site to a processing facility. Impurities can be removed and the oil can be sold and either trucked, pipelined, or sent by rail to its final destination.

Your royalty will be based on the sales price the company gets for the natural gas, oil, and/or any other products less the costs of gathering and processing the product(s). During lease negotiations, there should have been some discussion about what deductions are allowed and whether there is a maximum limit to these deductions. These should all be clearly stated on your lease. Your royalty will be paid monthly assuming that the well continues to produce. Your lease will also set out how soon after production your royalty should be paid.

If prices decline and it is no longer economic to produce the oil or gas, the company may decide to shut in production; i.e., stop producing the well until conditions improve. Think about it; why would a company want to keep producing a well at a low price if it is making minimal or negative returns? That is not in the best interests of its stakeholders, whether they are shareholders in the company or you, the mineral landowner with whom the company has a mineral lease. Since your royalty is based on the price the company receives, wouldn't you want them to produce and sell the product when prices are high rather than low? During the time that the well is shut in, most leases provide for a shut-in royalty payment or a suspended well payment.

Key Points in This Chapter

- If a company decides not to drill on your land, it may try to find another company to commit to doing so.

- Common agreements between companies include Joint Operating Agreements, Pooling Agreements, Farm-out or Farm-in Agreements, and Seismic Option Agreements.

- The agreements noted above are all a form of Joint Venture Agreement, but typically Joint Venture Agreements cover more land, have larger financial commitments, or simply have much more complex components or terms.

- The negotiating skill of the landmen and the relationships they have built up through their career can determine whether they are able to negotiate successful agreements for their companies.

9

When Land Changes Hands

JUST AS A surface landowner can sell their land or will it to children or siblings, a mineral landowner can sell or will their mineral rights. If the title is held with another party as joint tenants, when one party dies, that party's share will go to the surviving party. If the title is held with another party as tenants in common, when one party dies, that party's share goes to their estate or beneficiary named in a will.

Be aware that if you have a number of children and have decided to will your land to all of them, this could create difficulty in the future as individual portions or shares can become very small. Problems may arise if a company wishes to lease the land, since it has to contact all of the individual title owners to sign a lease with each of them. One possible method to deal with this, particularly if you want all of your heirs to share in the land, is to put the land into a corporation, with all heirs having shares in the company. Another possibility is to arrange for one of the heirs to act as a trustee for the other heirs. A number of different structures can be set up depending on your circumstances, the family dynamics, and the individuals involved. It is best to seek legal advice to find a solution that works for you and your heirs.

Whether you have sold the property or you have died and your heirs now have the land, it is very important that someone notify any company (Lessee) with which you had a lease. This is usually done through the lawyer handling the sales transaction or the lawyer or executor handling your estate.

Depending on where you or your heirs are located and where the land is located, the requirements to transfer the lease may differ. This is why it is wise to seek legal advice to ensure that the proper documentation is prepared, executed, and delivered to the Lessee so it can amend its records and send notices and payments to the correct individuals.

Key Points in This Chapter

- Seek legal advice to find the best way to pass your land on to someone else.

- With any change in land title, someone must notify the Lessee to ensure it has the correct current landholders and addresses on file.

10

Final Thoughts

THIS BOOK WAS meant to demystify the basic concepts of mineral land for the landowner and others interested in the oil and gas industry. Below are some of the key messages I want to leave with you.

- Know what land rights you own.

- Know what rights you are contracting. Think about your land in three dimensions, like a layer cake.

- An oil and gas lease is a contract.

- Understand the contract you are entering into and what your rights and obligations are.

- Once you have entered into a contract, keep up on what's happening to your land. It's your asset; no one should care more about it than you.

- With a Petroleum and Natural Gas Lease, the Lessee pays the Lessor for the right to find and remove petroleum substances by drilling a well. The Lessee does not have the obligation to drill.

- The Lessor and the Lessee are partners in the development of the land. The Lessor cannot make money from the land asset unless the Lessee makes money.

- If both parties understand the terms of the agreement and are happy with it because it benefits both, then that is a good deal.

- If you are going to hire someone to help you with your land issues, make sure that the person or company understands the issues from both sides.

- For landmen negotiating deals with other companies, the relationships they develop in the industry are critical to their success and the success of any company they work for.

While there are projects focused on developing alternative forms of energy, I suspect that the search for and production of fossil fuels will be around for some time. Until the cost to produce alternative forms of energy becomes competitive with the cost to produce oil and natural gas, companies do not have a lot of incentive to develop alternative forms and consumers do not have a lot of incentive to switch from oil and gas.

My time to date within the industry shows that the Western Canadian Sedimentary Basin keeps giving and giving.

Additional resources are produced almost every time a new technology is applied to this basin. It doesn't matter whether that new technology improves how we see the resource or how we produce the resource once it has been found. New technology is adding to our resource base in western Canada.

I hope you have found this book informative and that it makes you curious to find out more about this industry.

As the oil and gas industry continues to thrive in western Canada, it is worthwhile for landowners and others to understand mineral and other land rights so that they can remain active participants in the industry and benefit from the resources available to us.

Sources of Further Information

Alberta Energy (www.energy.gov.ab.ca)

This is the Government of Alberta department that deals with Crown lands. Here you can find information not only on Crown ownership of lands but also about the various resources in the province, energy legislation, maps, and the calculation of royalties on Crown lands.

Alberta Energy Regulator (www.aer.ca)

The Alberta Energy Regulator regulates oil and gas activity in the province. Besides outlining the process that companies need to go through, the website contains data about daily drilling activity, a map of abandoned wells, rules and directives that a company must follow, decisions of hearings, and advice on how to get involved in the exploration and production process, among other items.

Alberta Farmers' Advocate Office, Alberta Agriculture and Rural Development (www.agric.gov.ab.ca)

On the website home page for the Department of Agriculture and Rural Development, enter "Farmers' Advocate Office" in the search box and follow the links. The Farmers' Advocate Office primarily serves surface landowners, and its website has sections on rural consumer protection and rural opportunities, including in the oil and gas industry.

Alberta Surface Rights Board (www.surfacerights.gov.ab.ca)

This website, primarily of interest to surface landowners, describes the dispute resolution processes available to landowners and how to access them.

Canadian Association of Petroleum Land Administration (www.caplacanada.org)

This organization is committed to supporting the land administration profession. Typically these are the individuals that landowners interact with, as they are responsible for sending out payments associated with mineral and Surface Leases and making sure your contact information is correct. They are often a landowner's main point of contact within the oil and gas industry.

Canadian Association of Petroleum Landmen (www.landman.ca)

This organization is committed to enhancing the land profession. The website provides general information about what a landman does, standard form agreements, and other information to support the land profession.

Canadian Association of Petroleum Producers (www.capp.ca)

This is an industry-based organization for Canada's oil and natural gas producers whose website contains a lot of information that a landowner would find educational. Under the Library & Statistics tab is a Publications section that provides information on a variety of subjects. Under the Statistics section is a good historical summary of the petroleum industry in Canada called the *Statistical Handbook*.

Canadian Society for Unconventional Resources (www.csur.com)

As its name implies, this association supports the exploration and development of unconventional resources in Canada. Its website has a strong emphasis on the transfer of technical information among different groups. Under the Resources tab are fact sheets, booklets, presentations, and videos about these developing resources.

Freehold Owners Association (www.fhoa.ca)

This association represents landowners who own mineral rights. The website contains a number of self-explanatory topics that mineral landowners will find interesting.

Pembina Institute (www.pembina.org)

This organization focuses on protecting Canada's environment by advancing clean energy solutions. Under the

Publications tab are numerous publications addressing various energy issues and their impact on the environment and the economy. One publication that may be of interest to landowners is the second edition of *When the Oilpatch Comes to Your Backyard*, which you can find by entering the title in the search box on the home page or Publications tab.

Frequently Used Terms

Accounting Procedure, 111
Agreement to Acquire, 92-93, 95

Bonus consideration, 75-79, 92-93, 95, 97, 99

Compensatory royalty, 85, 88-89, 95
Conventional resources, 86-87
Cross conveyed pooling, 112
Crown, 4, 22-23, 31-33, 48, 50, 55
Crown land sale, 67, 77, 98-102

Deep rights reversion, 89, 91, 95
Delay rental, 83, 95, 106
Dominion Land Survey System (DLSS), 23
Downstream, 15, 19
Drilling spacing unit (DSU), 41, 45, 48, 85-86

Explorers and Producers, 7, 13, 17-19

Farmee, 114-116
Farmor, 114-116
Farm-out/Farm-in Agreement, 114-116, 122
Fee simple land (see freehold land), 23, 31-32
Formation, 30, 45, 61, 65, 69, 88-89, 104
Fractional interest, 70
Freehold land, 31, 67

Geologist, 12-14, 117
Geophysicist, 6, 117
Gross Royalty Trust (GRT) Agreement, 58, 79, 95

Horizon, 69, 84-85

Integration, 13, 15

Joint Operating Agreement, 111
Joint tenancy, 26
Joint Venture Agreement,
 119-120, 122

Land broker, 67, 70
Landman, 6, 75, 107-108, 116
Lessee, 65, 67, 83-85, 88, 112,
 124, 126
Lessor, 65, 67, 81, 83-84, 88, 112,
 115, 126

Mineral land rights, 3-4, 9-10,
 21, 113
Mineral lease, 46, 48, 63, 68-70,
 82, 89, 107, 121

Non-cross conveyed pooling, 112
Non-operator, 16-17

Offset well, 84-86, 88-89, 91, 95
Offsets, 84-88
Operating Procedure, 110-112
Operator, 16-17, 63, 66, 110-112
Option to Lease, 92-93, 95
Optionee, 92-93, 117-119
Optionor, 92-93, 116, 119

Pooling Agreement, 46, 63,
 111-112, 122
Pooling Order, 42, 47-48, 104, 112

Right-of-Way Agreement, 50, 52
Royalty, 46-48, 64-65, 77-85,
 88-89, 95, 115, 121

Seismic Option Agreement,
 116-119, 122
Seismic program, 117-119
Service Companies, 13, 16-19
Shut-in royalty, 95, 106, 121
Surface land rights, 26-27, 30-34,
 49-55, 61, 64
Surface Lease, 50-52, 55
Suspended well, 121

Tenancy in common, 26
Term, 76

Unconventional resources, 87, 131
Upstream, 15, 19

Working interest, 4, 8, 70, 111,
 115-116

About the Author

MS. LOUIE IS an oil and gas professional with over thirty-five years of experience in negotiations, government relations, business development, strategy development, mediation, and coaching. She has a Master of Business Administration, a Bachelor of Commerce, and a Bachelor of Science, all from the University of Calgary. She has been a member of the Canadian Association of Petroleum Landmen (CAPL) since 1980; she was granted the Professional Landman designation in 1990, and she served three terms on the board of the CAPL. A graduate of the Directors Education Program of the Institute of Corporate Directors, Ms. Louie was granted the ICD.D designation in 2011. She currently serves as a board member of Alberta Theatre Projects and the Calgary Convention Centre Authority.

CPSIA information can be obtained at www.ICGtesting.com
Printed in the USA
BVOW08s2018300416
445804BV00002B/49/P